"In today's world, culture is critical to your success as an organization. This fascinating book unveils an often overlooked part of developing a healthy and successful culture - the Power of Play. Companies like Southwest Airlines, Zappos and Google have pioneered this philosophy to great success and now every company culture will benefit from the ideas in this book."

TY BENNETT, author of The Power of Influence & The Power of Storytelling

"Despite my hectic & extensive schedule in the entertainment business, this book has taught me balance between having more fun and being productive at the same time. Thank You Russ for teaching my family and I how to enjoy and savor each moment despite our crazy lifestyles."

MERRILL OSMOND, Entertainer (The Osmonds), Two Grammy Award Nominations

"PLAY is a well thought-out and well-researched book in an important topic that can help companies thrive. The book synthesizes loads of research and bundles it up into an easily accessible package. It's a wonderful read for both those looking to gain buy-in from others in their organization and those wishing to implement play into their workplace."

SUE LANDAY, President - Trainers Warehouse and Office Oxygen

"A gem! When people have fun the creative sparks fly and interpersonal conflict disappears. The huge problem solved by Play is that most people, teams, and organizations have NO IDEA how to build this essential yet elusive ingredient into their DNA. This book is a blueprint for doing just that!"

MIKE SONG, Author | Zip! Tips: The Fastest Way to Get More Done

"Let this book shift your thinking as you take a more purposeful role in shaping the culture at your office. Whether you are the CEO or at the bottom of the org chart, make Play your work bible."

JASON ALBA, CEO of JibberJobber.com

PLAY

THE NEW LEADERSHIP SECRET THAT CHANGES EVERYTHING

RUSS JOHNSON

Copyright © 2014 Russ Johnson
First Edition
All rights reserved.

ISBN-13: 978-1499797053

Book Cover & Design by PIXEL eMarketing INC.

No part of this publication may be reproduced, stored in a retrieval system or transmitted in any form or by any means, electronic, mechanical, photocopying, recording, scanning or otherwise, except under the terms of the Copyright, Designs and Patents Act 1988 or under the terms of a license issued by the Copyright Licensing Agency Ltd.

Legal Disclaimer

The Publisher and the Author make no representations or warranties with respect to the accuracy or completeness of the contents of this work and specifically disclaim all warranties, including without limitation warranties for a particular purpose. No warranty may be created or extended by sales or promotional materials. The advice and strategies contained herein may not be suitable for every situation.

Neither the publisher nor the author shall be liable for damages arising herefrom. The fact that an organization or website is referred to in this work as a citation and/or a potential source of further information does not mean that the author or the publisher endorses the information the organization or website may provide or recommendations it may make.

Further, readers should be aware that Internet websites listed in this work may have changed or disappeared between when this work was written and when it is read.

I dedicate this book to you, the reader. Your willingness to awaken The Playful Leader within you is inspirational...to lead and inspire greatness by lightening up just a little and realizing the amazing results that come through states of productive play. Thank you for the investment you have made in you by purchasing and reading this book. You will see exciting results if you apply the principles.

And to my prize possession—my family!

Contents

Introduction: A Culture of Fun: The Art of Play at Work 1

Chapter 1: The Most Important Work We Do Is Play 5

Chapter 2: The Surprising Truth of Productive Play 17

Chapter 3: Play the King Atys Way 31

Chapter 4: The Seesaw Effect (Play Structures) 43

Chapter 5: Permission to Play Your Best Hand 63

Chapter 6: Discovering Your Company Playground 73

Chapter 7: Influencing and Connecting With Play 85

Chapter 8: Playing Hard With Organizational Change 101

Chapter 9: Leveling the Playing Field: Take Action! 111

Chapter 10: Too Serious to Be Happy (Taking It Home) 121

Chapter 11: Becoming The Playful Leader in a Serious World .129

Conclusion 156

References 159

About the Author 171

Introduction

A Culture of Fun: The Art of Play at Work

"Not everyone can be funny, but everyone can play!"

RUSS JOHNSON

With some of America's forward thinking companies benefitting from the "play" model, perhaps it is time to investigate exactly how "fun" is making a comeback in the world of business. So much more can be achieved when play is involved. Just look at companies like Uncharted Play.

These visionaries are positively influencing global social change using play. One of their flagship products—Soccket—is an energy harnessing soccer ball. As people play, kinetic energy is stored and can then be used as an off-the-grid power source in developing countries.

PLAY

Jessica Matthews and her team are using play to generate renewable energy. In much the same way, play can be used to generate energy within organizations to trigger a wide range of scientifically proven benefits that facilitate and improve working environments.

New research is surfacing all the time about the incredible benefits of designing play into your average work day. And the effects are far reaching—improving leadership, employee satisfaction and retention, creativity, and problem solving, and the list goes on!

There are playground moments for everyone looking to implement play into their corporate structure. These moments are where most of the benefits come from, and they are what this book is fundamentally about.

Lionel was a food service guy who worked at the Disney Yacht Club Resort in Orlando. Two days earlier, while presenting a keynote speech and delivering several other sessions, I learned that every morning a Disney character comes in and allows for photos with the participants.

One day it was Woody from Toy Story, and the next day it was Cinderella. On day three I was getting my breakfast and there was Lionel, the food service guy. He was creating buzz in a crowd of people, declaring, "Come get a photo with Goofy!" Participants sprung up to get a photo with Lionel the food guy because he was creating his own playground moment.

The data screams that play leads to increased productivity! When leaders lighten up and create a fun workplace environment, there is a significant increase in the level of employee trust, creativity, and communication, which leads to lower turnover, higher morale, and a stronger bottom line. May we allow The Playful Leader inside us to ignite a new culture of productivity through the spirit of purposeful fun.

People love to play, and it has been marginalized for too long in corporate business culture. This book will help orient you in the new research of play and how it can contribute to building amazing business cultures like the ones you see at Google, Southwest Airlines, and Zappos. Lighten up, sit back, and prepare for the serious world of play!

01

The Most Important Work We Do Is Play

> "What do most Nobel Laureates, innovative entrepreneurs, artists and performers, well-adjusted children, happy couples and families, and the most successfully adapted mammals have in common? They play enthusiastically throughout their lives."
>
> **STUART BROWN, INSTITUTE OF PLAY**

When I started my journey investigating the wide world of play, I quickly realized that there was a lot of work to be done. There were misconceptions running rampant and an increasing body of evidence that suggest the companies that play hard succeed.

If you have ever stepped into the Zappos offices, you would wonder how any work gets done. Cow bells ring out, people with Nerf guns fly around corners chasing each other—it is more than a circus; it is chaos. So why is Zappos one of the most successful online retailers in the world? The work gets done, yet people play!

The History and State of Play in the Workplace

There are huge differences between a "play"-oriented company and your average company here in the U.S. Walk into Zappos and you will find the most elaborately decorated cubicles—space aliens, surfing, a 1950s theme on the corner. Behind it, a team of people wearing party hats play ring toss.

Walk into another company in the same office block, and the silence is deafening. Everything is wood and grey and stiff. No one laughs; no one plays. This is the corporate America we have all come to accept. Business is business, and it is *serious*. But why?

When you are doing something fun—without a goal or a purpose—that is the state of play. Becoming deeply engaged in these states brings a sense of playfulness into an otherwise drab office environment. When something is new and exciting, or if it is risky, it creates a rush of excitement that can be insanely fun.

Playful organizations thrive because they reject the notion that business has to be serious all the time. When you play in the moment or create what I call "playground moments," you stand to benefit from it in all sorts of incredible ways.

Zappos was ranked as one of the best places in the country to work. Not only did their culture of play not harm their bottom line, it improved it. Zappos made more than a billion dollars in sales last year. For most other shoe retailers, this is a pipe dream.

When you can let go and offer employees a chance to be who they truly are, the response is overwhelming. Everyone smiles, and everyone works hard when it matters. State of play is an attitude, a state of mind. It means to "work in the spirit of play."

Productive play is a vision that more companies should be embracing. It is a way of connecting, reaching out to people, and reaching inside yourself. When everyone is happy and moving in the same direction towards a common goal, magic happens.

Common Dollars and Cents: Approaching Play

While in Seattle speaking to the teams at Microsoft, I started by introducing myself: "My mascots are the Cougar and the Thunderbird. Any guesses where I went to college?" Someone shouted, "Washington State!" I said no. Then BYU was mentioned and "that international business school" in Phoenix.

I nodded. The American Graduate School of International Management. "And I have one more mascot...the Bronco!" Half the room erupted into melodic boos, with a quiet "yea" somewhere near the back.

The Seattle Seahawks had just beaten the San Francisco 49ers a week before in an absolutely thrilling NFC Championship game. Media hype was building for the upcoming Super Bowl. Suddenly, executives were sitting on the edge of their seats. "Just kidding!" I added in, but I had their attention now.

Play is not a word that is used much in the corporate world. I mean, how do you measure play's return on investment? Some people say that you cannot place a numeric value on it. That "fun" still has a powerful role to play in the business world.

Play can do a lot for progressive companies looking for a way to make their employees work harder and their customers happier. Approaching play is not about disorganization; it is about understanding the role that fun has in the life of a human being.

- Theodore Roosevelt was a play advocate and stated that kids need it to develop properly, otherwise a life of crime waits. He mentioned that play was a fundamental need and instinctual to human nature.
- Gamification is on the rise with the basic theory that "if you can make something more fun by including play, you can get more people to do things they might not want to do," says Gabe Zichermann.

Traditionally, work and play are thought of as separate or off-site activities. Loads of workers still feel that playing on the job is a sin. With global competition on the rise and every penny making the difference in business, a happy employee is of paramount importance.

What makes employees happy? Play! An atmosphere of playfulness is transformative, but you have to approach it in a methodical way or chaos will ensue! A big part of this book is orienting you in "what play is" and then helping you find structure to initiate productive play.

When you can cultivate a spirit of playfulness among your teams, the pain of monotony will vanish. Boredom, repetition, and mundane work will be replaced with high energy, outside-of-the-box thinking and creative solutions.

Fun, as research indicates, is particularly useful during difficult economic times. Employees are asked to do more with less, and "play" can balance out the stress of it all! Clearly when it comes to dollar and cents, the real "sense" is found in play.

Play Dead: Two Dangerous Myths About Play

I once bought a book at Barnes and Noble called *Be a Great Stand-Up*. Now, I have no ambition to be a comedian or a stand-up comic, but the subject matter looked fun, and I am always looking for new ways to find playful engagement. When I approached the front desk and the clerk rang up my book, he said, "Good luck with that!"

In response, I frowned deeply. "What is the matter? Do I not look like a funny guy?" Realizing he may have just dashed my dreams, he was quick to apologize profusely. "No offense taken," I said, switching my face back to a broad smile. We traded knowing looks—I had just playfully tricked him into thinking I was upset over his jab. We connected.

Why are people so ready to switch back and forth between being playful and being serious? There are two very dangerous myths about play that you need to know about. This book will go a long way in reprogramming that out of you!

- *Myth 1:* It is impossible to play and be productive. This is a horrible lie. Whoever made this rule was not thinking clearly. People are conditioned to be serious and to stifle any fun or humor on the job. When play scenarios arise, they can barely participate because of this debilitating belief. Play at work, and bad things will happen. Do not mess around at work! You will get fired! All myths.
- *Myth 2:* Play costs the company money. Really? What about places like Zappos, Google, and Facebook? There is a cost involved with play, but it is the cost of a disengaged employee. A sense of humor is a sense of perspective. People can take their work seriously and themselves lightly.

A huge body of evidence supports the idea that a "fun workplace" fixes the "grumpy" employee problem. Michael Ema, a professor of psychology at Larene CN University, is also a standup comic. It is an odd combo, yes, but a solid attempt at work–life balance.

Most people have to face the reality that their jobs are relentlessly boring. Productive play can help you and your organization.

The word is out! Employees that enjoy their jobs work harder and are more efficient than the employees who do not. Companies are re-examining their old ideals because of this. Disengaged employees cost companies billions of dollars. The fact is that play is business relevant, it improves productivity, and it plugs a gaping hole that has been around too long.

Why You Feel Bad About Feeling Good

In my seminars, I do an activity called "opposites." When I use this teaching activity, I ask my audience to repeat the opposite of the word that I say. I start with a word like "tall." The audience replies "short." Then we move through heavy, light, dark, light, sad, happy. Eventually, I say "play." The response? Work!

This is *not* the accurate opposite of play. In fact, work and play are inclusive.

The new business environment is forcing employees to do more with less and to gain knowledge at a faster rate. People tend to treat humor like it is an emergency. Even Isaac Asimov once said the most exciting thing to hear in science is not "Eureka!" It's "That's funny."

Traditional wisdom tells us work is not supposed to be fun; that is why it is called work. The other end of this is if you see someone having fun at work, it means that they are slacking off. Slacking off leads to the company losing money. You get fired. In Western society, this has translated into the stiff, no-play corporate lifestyle.

When people are relaxed, energized, and having fun, they are at their best. Plato said, "All learning has an emotional base." What better learning environment than one in which play is glorified so that employees can step onto the playground and expand their thinking without fear of losing their jobs or getting into trouble?

We are living in the era of collaboration, where managers trust their employees instead of policing and micro managing them. If you learn to give the power back to your employees so that they can express fun and play in constructive ways, it will destroy those conditioned feelings of "slack off–get fired" that their parents drummed into them.

Who Says Play and Work Don't Work?

How do you feel after going through security and putting yourself back together? In Milwaukee, they call it a "recombobulation area"—it fits, and it is fun. The experience helps passengers recover from a stressful experience and serves the airline's purpose. Passengers smile as they see the sign hanging at concourse C.

Dr. Brown of the Play Institute says that "the most important work we do is play." There is so little of it in corporate America, and that has to change! There is very real ROI involved with instituting play policy at work.

The proof is in the profit, employee productivity boosts, and widespread effects across the entire organization. To be more productive at work, people should play.

When you play, it generates energy in people, and it is this energy that is used to work. Play engages employees, and they need to be engaged more often. A Gallup poll indicated that most employees are horrendously disengaged.

You need to recharge your organization through structured, methodical play. Google's success is directly related to fun. The physical work space offers a culture of play—there are sharing cubes, pianos, and slides that make up the offices. Each work environment is distinct, incorporating some local flair.

This is done to keep employees happy and to create an innovative and creative environment that people can work in. Zappos takes play very seriously. After screening their job applicants, they offer them one month salary to leave. The choice becomes, embrace our culture of play and work for us, or take the money and run.

Noel Dyck, professor of social anthropology at Simon Fraser, advocates that people wrongly believe that only childhood is meant to be playful. But a balance needs to be struck between the mechanics and structure of the game—so that it can be played for fun.

Do you sometimes wish that you could play video games at work? Or have a drink there? Or exercise there? Global companies are integrating these employee wishes into their daily lives. Encouraging play boosts morale, fosters increased creativity and work alignment, and brings teams closer together.

Accountemps did a survey and discovered that 96% of execs think that people with a sense of humor do better in their jobs than people with no sense of humor. America's hottest companies are playing and earning non-stop. Work needs to be fun, and this is reflected in Forbes "hundred best companies to work for" list.

Proof That Play Is the Missing Link

Zappos, as a company, and Tony Hsieh, the company CEO, are making incredible waves in the field of play and work.

ZAPPOS FAMILY CORE VALUES

As we grow as a company, it has become more and more important to explicitly define the core values from which we develop our culture, our brand, and our business strategies. These are the ten core values that we live by:

1. Deliver WOW Through Service
2. Embrace and Drive Change
3. Create Fun and a Little Wierdness
4. Be Adventerous Creative and Open- Minded
5. Pursue Growth and Learning
6. Build Open and Honest Relationships with Communication
7. Build a Positive Team and Family Spirit
8. Do More with less
9. Be Passionate and Determined
10. Be Humble

There are economics involved in play as an essential element in business. Far beyond its social virtues, play makes companies money. Zappos' revenue grew from $1.6 million in 2000 to $1.6 billion in 2010. "It's a brand about happiness, whether to customers, or employees, or even vendors," said Tony Hsieh.

Each department head is expected to spend 10–20% of their time on employee team building opportunities. The employees become integrated and comfortable with the culture and with each other. They develop deep relationships and are better able to collaborate, share, and engage with each other in the work place.

The same is happening with Southwest Airlines. CEO Herb Kelleher has said on more than one occasion that they hire "attitudes," not people.

There is no denying that happy workers are productive workers. If you are not having fun at work, you are not employing the latest organizational strategy that promotes productivity and change. Motivating and retaining employees is important—and there are so few ways to do that in the non-play business world.

Play has been the missing link for so many companies that have now made the switch. Remember that recombobulation area? That was a tactic employed by Milwaukee's Mitchell International Airport. In the spirit of fun, passengers could step out of the line and fix themselves after the security checkpoint search.

It turned a horrible experience into something that was taken less seriously—and this defused line tension and reduced pressure on the airline customers. These examples prove that playful leadership has perhaps been the single most important thing that has been missing from corporate America for so many years. Hopefully it will return like a caped crusader!

Playground Days: What They Should Have Taught You

Yum! On May 30, 1997, a new brand was launched called Yum. Yum brands put fast-food yummies in a whole lot of tummies. They are the world's largest fast food operator, and they send a playful signal by what could otherwise be some stuffy corporate verbiage. The name says it all.

When I realized that I could play—and still work hard—my life changed. Gallup recently reported that more than 52% of all U.S. workers are not engaged in their work. That means they were not committed, not loyal, and not particularly interested in their jobs. Scary!

But is it their fault or the fault of the company? Disengaged employees cost companies $550 billion every year from productivity losses. These people are more likely to steal, to negatively influence co-workers, and to drive customers away.

Remember the playground at school? You could play there, and you were free to jump, create, pretend, and explore. This playground was built to allow kids to do this, but it was also built for coordination improvement, motor skills, and imaginative development as well as to allow the teachers to take a break.

Play structures link different types of equipment to form playgrounds. Organized play areas have been around since 1859. Playground social skills are vital, and they help kids develop healthily through spontaneous play. Mastering physical skills, developing personally, and improving communication are all things that still need to happen in your adult years!

Every company has its own unique cultural considerations. Fun on the job does not have to equal humor or silliness. You do not need to be as extreme as Zappos with Nerf guns or as innovative as Google with slides.

Tom Sawyer, in the famous Mark Twain classic, becomes

bored when whitewashing a fence. He sees it as work, so he turns it into a game by convincing his friends to do it. The work gets done, and Tom achieves his goal.

Your old playground days should have taught you that getting to know people—and yourself—is instrumental in collaborative environments. You should have realized that doing "mindless" tasks stimulates big idea thinking and creative input.

New Rules of Playground Engagement

Your work environment should emulate the playgrounds from your childhood. You will need a roadmap for developing business playground structures and a method of testing if they are bringing out the best in your employees.

Do not take yourself and your organization so seriously. If you want to play your way to increased profits, you have to work on your existing business culture. First of all, learn to energize your organization through play, and use it as a tool to point people in the right direction. This is how you begin to reorganize your culture. Here are some rules!

- Fun is an atmosphere! It is not so much something you do or create. It is a state of mind. It is an attitude. It is an approach to work.
- Learn how to trigger a playful atmosphere that connects people. That means formulating playground rules and boundaries. Nothing lightens up the brain like play. Not everyone can be funny, but everyone can play.
- California State University has proven that people who work with fun in mind are more creative and productive and are sick less often.
- Fun at work can lead to the alleviation of boredom that arises from dull, routine, and non-challenging tasks.

- Leadership will be the reason your company thrives. Do not be afraid to take risks; the bigger risk is allowing people to remain bored in their jobs! A positive, effective company culture can cure most organizational concerns. The missing element is play!
- Company culture should be the sum of the "hearts" of your people. Entertain, educate, and sell with humor and play in mind. It always gets people's attention.
- Recharge your batteries with play. A playful leader is one that stands apart from the rest and is not afraid to harness new ideas to improve business.

If you are going to become The Playful Leader, then these are the concerns and concepts that you have to play with. Play should be a part of innovative business culture if you want to step into the modern world and make people happy.

02

The Surprising Truth of Productive Play

"If you have fun at what you do, you'll never work a day in your life. Make work like play—and play like hell."

NORM BRINKER

Productive play, as I like to call it, is the key to plugging that "seriousness" gap that continues to undermine your business culture. Now, there are many reasons to shy away from "play" as an element of your business—but many more that indicate it is the right thing to do.

The "stereotype of play" can make you blind and deaf to all of the potential possibilities that you could invite into your business culture. This chapter will outline exactly why "play" is an elusive buzzword in the business arena right now.

The Call to Play: Why You Need to Listen

Bob Pike, author of *The Fun Minute Manager,* advocates a fun working environment where formal and informal activities occur regularly in order to light people's spirits and remind them of their value to managers.

He goes on to mention that through humor, games, and celebrations, there are unique opportunities to learn and grow as a person. There is a call to play inside every person who works for you. They long for it on weekends or when they see their friends. The work you give them makes them feel like those "good times" are few and far between.

Let's get something straight here! Seriousness is *not* the same as professionalism. Professionalism is about doing your job well and treating others with respect. Work and play are not opposites; they are part of the same whole (the individual!).

- When people have fun, they work harder. They stay longer, and they maintain their composure in a crisis more efficiently than if they do not play at work.

Kirt Womack[1] works in the Thiokol factory in Utah. On the first day of spring, he asked his manager if they could go outside and do something fun if they finished their quota two hours early that day. He proposed flying paper airplanes. The manager said no. Kirt continued to argue his point and asked if it would be possible if they exceeded their quota by 50%.

Finally, the boss agreed because he believed it would be impossible. By 1:30, 100% of the work was done. By 3 p.m., 50% more work was done. The airplanes were launched, and people loved it.

The 50% increase was followed by a boost in employee happiness. It was a risk and reward system that worked. The

---

[1] Adrian Gostick & Scott Christopher, The Levity Effect: Why It Pays to Lighten Up

promise of fun can be a powerful thing, and employees are always up for it. The next week they had an employee volleyball game. The factory floor produced record breaking levels of production. That is powerful play!

Word Play: Improving Sales and Communications

One of the most impressive returns that play offers The Playful Leader is the opportunity to improve sales and communication. They are both linked to so many outcomes for a business.

If you want to improve sales, then you need to improve communication. If you want people to connect on an authentic level, you have to make it fun! Gartner predicts that by 2015 some 40% of global organizations will use "gamification" as a primary method of transforming business operations for their employees.

Fun affects so many things: higher job satisfaction, employee morale, pride in work, creativity, customer service—all of it. Contrast this against anxiety, social ineptitude, tardiness, burnout, and absenteeism, and the ROI is amazing.

Employees born in 1980 that are part of the millennial generation need play even more than their baby boom counterparts. Customer complaints will decrease if you have a happy workforce—fact! Your employees will look forward to coming to work when they can play a little—fact! They will work hard to achieve goals if they can play—fact!

Sales is a uniquely social game to be in, and it benefits enormously from role-playing experiences, games, and other forms of development and rehearsal. Productive play can improve the overall sales of the team by allowing people to grow, ask questions, and experience new tactics in a real-world context.

This play will help your team connect with clients, and it will give them the energy that they need to provide excellent customer service, to think creatively, and to come up with solutions that will ultimately benefit your business. This is the real benefit of adding fun to your business culture. Front-line sales teams will love it, and it will help them connect, share, and collaborate in new and interesting ways. All you have to do is give them a chance—basically by example and permission.

Playing to Win: Improving Leadership and Productivity

Two of the most critical aspects in business these days are leadership and productivity. In fact, leaders that can make their employees more productive are highly sought after. It is good news then that fun improves work productivity.

According to Steve Wilson, a 15% morale boost becomes a 40% increase in productivity. That is a staggering statistic when you consider that improving morale is not something that is ever really on the minds of managers. Work forces are on a "productivity sliding scale," but the basic missing element is playful leadership (on the lower end of the scale).

When a leader introduces new methods of play into the workplace, it almost always leads to an instant increase in productivity. People have gotten into bad habits and bad mindsets about work. They have labelled their jobs and their careers as "work," and this has crowded out all other forms of logic.

The notion that you are supposed to grow as a human being, for example, always takes a back seat to profit. That is why this link between play and profit is astonishing. Clearly, the work force in America is so disillusioned with their jobs that they are ready to do anything and everything to mix things up.

Gallup conducted research involving 17 million employees on emotional commitment to company goals. Actively disengaged employees cost companies in America $300 billion every year. Performance, engagement, and retention skyrocket when employees have fun.

Leaders can use play as a competitive advantage to drive organizational change and improve performance. A survey of 329 companies found that 97% of leaders agreed that humor was valuable in business. Some 84% of employees do better at work when they have a sense of humor on their side.

With people spending more time at work, integration with play is essential. Having fun at work can include any social, interpersonal, or job-related activity that a person finds enjoyable and interesting. Your job will be to design these experiences and demonstrate this attitude for your teams.

Playful Innovation: Increasing Retention and Creativity

So play has a lot of benefits for leaders and employees. Two of the most impressive benefits are retention and creativity. Because play alters behavior and improves the employee's ability to learn, it is also an invaluable learning tool.

- *Play increases employee retention*: In a recent study conducted by teams from Penn State, Loyola University of Maryland and Ohio State University, 195 restaurant workers were asked some questions. The restaurant industry is notorious for low retention rates—so the study was set. The results were clear: fun activities and manager support for fun improve retention rates and sale performance.
- *Play increases innovation and creativity*: At LinkedIn, the business networking giant, employees can play ping

pong and foosball when they need a break. At Zynga, the popular app company, employees can play arcade games. Ambient noise, music, and fun with other employees always improve creativity and innovative thinking.

- ***Play increases company morale***: An atmosphere of play raises people's spirits, and they do not feel trapped. The "work hard, play hard" model has been used for years, yet it has not surfaced until recently. Company employees that play together feel like they belong to the culture of the company and gain an appreciation for their job, their colleagues, and their bosses. Morale is improved!
- ***Play fosters a greater sense of teamwork in people***: When people can experience things together during play, they connect on a deeper level. In today's workplace, limited interactions lead to disjointed teams. When you invite play into your team building experiences, everyone benefits.

Perceived workplace fun has a positive impact on applicant attraction to certain jobs as well. As an employee recruitment strategy, it works! Just look at Google and how hard people fight for a chance to work there.

This is because they understand that Google will offer them so much more than any other company in terms of personal growth, satisfaction, and fun.

This Is Your Brain on Play

Nothing lights up the human brain more than when it is in play mode. When you and your team have entered a "state of play," there are neurological effects that are hugely beneficial. The one in particular that I want to point out is happiness.

According to the Mayo Clinic, pessimists die younger than optimists. A study of 839 patients in 1960 involving detailed personality tests and the optimism–pessimism scale resulted in the conclusion that optimists outlive pessimists.

This is an amazing statistic considering that optimism is also responsible for improved concentration and performance. And because optimism is directly linked to workplace satisfaction, it gives you—the leader—an excellent opportunity.

If you can use play to improve your employees' "outlook" and make them more optimistic about their work than pessimistic, it will rapidly increase concentration and performance and contribute to happier, healthier people in your organization.

Thoughts can change the function of your brain—and thoughts are influenced predominantly by external influences, like where you work and how your average day goes. Employees that enjoy playtime during work are happier because over time, they learn to adopt a more positive mindset.

This limits negative thinking like fear of failure and worry and even curbs things like mood disorders. Neuroplasticity is so powerful that doctors are experimenting with it to cure things like chronic pain, hearing disorders, loss of senses, and cognitive disorder.

In this sense, when you institute and drive a culture of play at work, you are actively reprogramming your employees' brains to be happier. This will reduce your medical costs, time taken off work, and loss of productivity—not to mention the dozens of positive side effects that happier people are able to enjoy.

This is the ultimate form of investment for your company. The results do not lie—employees that work for progressive companies using play as an organizational tool are happier and healthier. They stay at these companies for longer because of this.

In this way, play begins a happiness cycle that improves so many features of the average modern day business. Team work, collaboration, independent thinking, and creativity all add up to produce a happier mind.

No More Funny Business: Chosen Benefits

THE 7 AMAZING BENEFITS OF PLAY

1. *Increased Productivity*
2. *Improved Communication*
3. *Greater Influence*
4. *Increased Innovation*
5. *Increased Company Morale*
6. *Greater Teamwork*
7. *Increased Profitability*

Employees are expected to act against human nature. They are told to show up on time, to get serious and be productive all day long, and to save their lighter side for breaks and after-hour time. Work and happiness are completely separated.

This may be the classical approach to play, but it interferes and detracts from productivity. The "no more funny business" mentality has got to go! Managers that act like police officers keeping prisoners working in their seats—no one wants to work like that.

The questions are: Can humor boost productivity? Should companies use humor to expand their bottom line? Can laughter help firms retain key talent? Adrian Gostick and Scott Christopher say yes to all three. They wrote a book called *The Levity Effect: Why It Pays To Lighten Up*, and their argument is clear: fun works.

A company that values humor can spark creativity when they need it. They can attract and retain super-employees that are highly talented. They can grab that competitive advantage when it matters most to their bottom line. This is a kind of super power that harnesses enjoyment, fun, and play and then converts it into very real business returns.

People that advocate for workplace fun say that when individuals are having fun at work, they are more energized and motivated. With this increased energy and motivation, there is also a rise in focus, dedication, and commitment to business objective achievement.

- With 88% of Millennials saying that they would prefer it if their colleagues were their friends, business needs to take a serious look at this light-hearted phenomenon.
- Happy employees stay longer hours, work harder, share with your company on its social media pages, and invite talented people they know to work for you.
- Fun in the workplace makes employees feel valued and recognized. This in turn motivates them to go above and beyond for your company.
- Decision making improves when employees are happier. And when decisions are being made in a state of happiness, the positive mindset will ensure that the goals or directives are met.
- There are increased levels of enthusiasm for employees that work in companies that focus on play in their organization.

The line has been drawn in the proverbial sand. In the future, there will be companies that are focused on employee happiness, fun, and play—and companies that do not care (or do not know). The world will be split in two, with the greatest talent heading off to the fun companies.

The only way that you as a leader will be able to affect your bottom line in the most positive manner is to institute play while it is still getting off the ground. This "funny business" is actually very serious business when you consider the momentum being gained in its widespread adoption in the U.S.

Unlocking Creative Energy With Fun

Play advocates are seeing additional benefits of a playful work culture. These are the virtues of play that go unseen when play is too badly limited in a corporation.

- Exercise in any form promotes circulation, and this, by its very nature, provokes creative thinking. Sometimes the best ideas come to you when you are doing something other than work. This is because the brain continues to think of the solution subconsciously.
- Human connection and the ability to brain swarm ideas collectively in a strong team environment are priceless. It is how they do it for sitcoms and movie scripts because not all ideas are great ideas. Your team will be able to easily sift through the junk ideas and settle on great ones much faster as they get to know each other.
- When creative energies like these are unleashed, dopamine—the "happy" chemical in the brain—(along with serotonin) is released. This neurotransmitter is closely related to motivation and creativity. Motivation comes from anticipation, not reward—play facilitates anticipation to work. While this is happening, dopamine is released and causes a surge of creativity. Then you sit down and go to work!
- When employees can "let go" and play, it instantly transforms the way they feel. A depressed emotional state can transform into a relaxed one. A closed mind can become open.

- Play connects employees with people, and sharing laughter, joy, and ideas builds a sense of community—which is essential to creative collaboration. Flexibility, learning, and perseverance are also affected because play opens people up to new experiences.

Play does unleash creative energy, but the real reward is when you notice that your teams really care about each other. This single factor will lead to greater consideration, kept deadlines, real effort, and bigger ideas being pushed through your teams.

The Neuroscience of Play

There is a lot of neuroscience involved in the art of play. Why are funny sales people better at selling than normal sales people? Because they invoke the release of dopamine in their clients, which makes them more susceptible to the pitch.

Take this joke for example: "Last winter, it was so cold that I actually saw a lawyer with his hands in his own pockets."

Pretty amusing, right? There is a reason for that.

Humor is a positive thing. Defined, it can be broken down into three distinct areas: emotional reaction, positive emotion of amusement, and cognitive reaction. Chemically, it is because of those neurotransmitters like adrenaline and dopamine that cause the response.

Adrenaline is made when people feel excitement, anger, frustration, and fear. It rapidly increases alertness. Oxytocin is a hormone that is strongly associated with fun. If you can engage your senses, it will be released.

Add adrenaline and oxytocin to dopamine and you have a cocktail for success. It means energy, morale, engagement, and more goodwill towards your company. This transformative force all comes from the simple act of playing.

- Fun loosens structured cognition, making things easier to learn. They say it triggers feel-good brain chemicals like the ones mentioned above. Positive and relaxed emotions flood your body. Finally, fun helps you to explore without fear of failure because there are no repercussions for your actions.
- Adrian Gostick and Scott Christopher have it right when they explain through interviews, case studies, and exercises that humor in the workplace helps build camaraderie, increases productivity, enhances employee satisfaction, and encourages creativity and innovation—all directed at helping the company make more money.
- Microsoft employees blast music at three in the afternoon when energy is low. Some people get up and dance or clap, and it shakes off the cobwebs. At LEGO, employees are allowed to travel around on their scooters.
- Companies that are classified as "great" score high marks from employees when their work environment is fun. Good companies come in at 62%, while great companies rank at 81%. This is a telling statistic! Employees want a fun work place!
- A study of 737 chief executives found that 98% of them would hire an applicant with a good sense of humor over one that lacked it.

When you increase individual engagement at work, everyone begins working towards the ultimate goal of the company. Race, generation, culture—all of that stuff falls away when people embrace their company culture.

Stress Reduction and Humor: The Facts

There are no greater tools in the world than humor and fun to reduce the effects of stress and anxiety. In today's insanely busy workplace, stress is a serious concern. Think about all of those times people are forced to stay late and earn less while the economy becomes less stable and more risky. Something has to give.

What "gives," in this instance, is stress. Employees are overloaded with it on a 24/7 basis. The more they play in your business environment, the more stress they will be able to relieve. When your office is an exciting place to work, people will want to get there as soon as possible because it becomes a "stress reliever" instead of an aggravator.

- Research shows that fun motivates employees to work longer and produce more. But it also helps workers deal with difficulties, stress, and the pressures of modern day living. Fun at work that gets the stress down is a health bonus.
- When the stress is taken out or reduced from your average work day, people's energy is increased, and they feel less lethargic about who they work for. In fact, pride sneaks in when employees become relaxed and happy at work.
- Laughter releases endorphins that are way more powerful than morphine. This leads to a persistent feeling of optimism and well-being. Employees that feel happier are not as stressed. Plus, the physical activity of moving around during play in their normal work day does a lot to lower their cortisol levels.
- Work can be hectic—with performance deadlines, quality reviews, and job competition. This all vanishes when there is a strong business culture that promotes fun in the workplace.

Stress causes burnout, a condition that forces an employee to take a few days or weeks off because they are exhausted. Over the last several years—due to high pressure and demand—burnout has become common.

Your company can eliminate the threat of burnout by engaging with your employees, using fun as a reason to do it. Humor changes the game, and it makes everything better for your employees and your customers and their mounting stress levels.

Laughing All the Way to the Bank

A savvy manager will always look at the data. In this instance, the data is perfectly clear. You can cash in on having more fun. It can be a tough sell to higher ups, but run a few internal tests to prove it, and you can make your career a fun, rewarding one.

- When you create a fun, play-based business culture, you will literally laugh all the way to the bank. This is because when your employees are happy, your customers are happy. This means that internally and externally, the structure of your company will be more solid—which will make your investors happy.
- Building playground structures into your daily work life is exactly the kind of extreme, outside-the-box thinking that you need to do. Use my exercise called "opposites" to enlighten your senior department heads. Tell them all to shout out what the opposite of play is, and then when they respond with "work," you can make changes.
- There is no doubt in my mind that play has its place among the highest earning companies in America right now. They have found a way to harness the playful mindset to improve work culture and processes across the board. The last time anything was so transformative, it was technology.

Think about the ways that your company can institute this invaluable organizational structure.

The proof, as they say, is in the profit. The funny thing is that when employees love their company, so do customers. It becomes a group happiness effort that can propel your profits into the big leagues! Do not ignore it!

03

Play the King Atys Way

"When we talk about the great workers of the world we really mean the great players of the world."

MARK TWAIN

Game play has been a critical part of human development for thousands of years. The first written history of human gameplay dates back to Herodotus 3000 years ago.

Herodotus recorded the cultural functions of play at these early games, and they can teach us a lot about why play is important in the business world today.

The Four Dimensions of Play (Herodotus Model)

To understand the four dimensions of play, you must first understand the story of King Atys. In the opening book of the Histories, Herodotus writes:

> "The Lydians themselves say that the games now in practice among themselves and the Greeks were their special invention. In the time of King Atys, the son of Manes, there was a severe famine throughout all Lydia. The Lydians bore it at first with patience, but thereafter, when it did not cease, they sought for remedies; one man would devise this and another that. And it was thus, that the games of dice, and the bones, and the ball, and the varieties of all other games were invented... They made the discovery of games against the famine, they say. For they would play the whole of every other day that they might not seek food in it, and then, the next day, they would give over their games and eat. So, according to the story, they managed to live for 18 years. But when their troubles grew no less, the King at last divided all the people of Lydia into two halves and cast lots, for the one half that should remain in the homeland and the other to immigrate. For the part they should draw the lot to remain, he appointed himself to be king; but for the one that should leave the country, he appointed his son, whose name was Tyrrhenus. They sailed away in quest of a country and a livelihood. They passed many nations by, in their progress, and came to Umbrians. There they established cities, and there they live till this day. From being called Lydians they changed their name: in honor of that son of their king who led them out, they called themselves, after him, Tyrrhenians."

By seeing play through the eyes of King Atys, we can see that play is supposed to be a strategic business lesson that teaches us about survival and organizational excellence. Play makes work—or any hardship—bearable. It gave the people something to do when all they could think about was hunger and starvation.

Herodotus looked back and knew that the games were an attempt to alleviate suffering. Ancient games were designed to make citizens more resilient. In a social crisis, games were a great way to intervene. To this day the power of productive play gives the people that use it an evolutionary advantage. King Atys taught us the following:

- Play on certain days, and eat on others. Play facilitates organization.
- Communicate problems to the people. Be creative about solutions.
- Some ideas work; some do not. Get everyone involved to find the solution.
- Leadership is imperative for productive play. Different levels of playful leaders must exist!
- Create better rules of engagement, and give permission for all to thrive through play.
- Play helps us coordinate our efforts and attitudes and helps us tackle any kind of challenge that is put in front of us.
- Play leads to reinvention, collaboration, and improved business culture.

Play Matrix Model

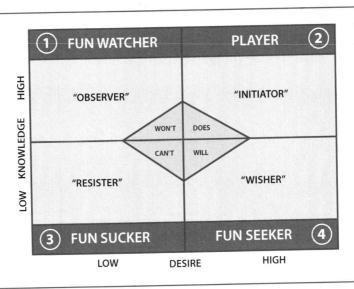

PLAY

I created the Play Matrix Model to help visually see what is going on at the game of work—who is involved and who is not playing at all. Let's keep playing.

In the Play Matrix Model that I use, there are four dimensions of productive play.

1. *Find Play in the System:* Find out where you can play and how.
2. *Give Permission to Play:* Give the people permission to play.
3. *Pursue Productive Play:* Find out ways of improving/using productive play.
4. *Extend Play Boundaries:* Get as many people as possible to play.

The dimensions govern play styles, roles, and characteristics, which I will discuss in more detail.

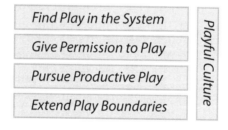

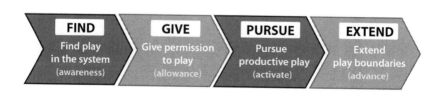

The Serious Act of Having Fun

There are very real correlations between becoming a playful leader and the rules that King Atys of Lydia put in place to save his kingdom. While these rules are old, the models have been tested over and over again by many different cultures (and some organizations).

King Atys of Lydia	The Playful Leader
"They Sought for Remedies"	Find Play in the System
"Games Against the Famine"	Give Permission to Play
"Play Every Other Day"	Pursue Productive Play
"Who Led Them Out"	Extend Play Boundaries

In the above comparison chart, you can see how the story of King Atys fits in perfectly with the four dimensions of productive play. Alongside this model is your company culture. Clearly, having a fun time is a very serious act, and we should all treat it that way.

The Play Matrix Model involves four quadrants that run along a knowledge and desire scale. The scale can then be broken down into the following areas:

- *The fun watcher:* This person is an observer that knows how to play but will not.
- *The player:* This person is an initiator and does play already.
- *The fun sucker:* This person is a resister and does not know how to play nor has any desire to.
- *The fun seeker:* This person is a wisher and wants to play but does not know how.

While on a recent water skiing trip with my married brothers and their kids at Utah Lake, my son introduced me to an interesting term. We had started skiing early with two boats, so by mid-afternoon the young ones were already bored of water tubing and being dragged behind the boats. My eldest turned to me and asked, "What about you, Dad?"

"What do you mean, what about me?" I asked in response. "Nice try. It's your turn," he said. "My turn to what?" I said, slightly alarmed. "Get on the water tube!" he yelled. And that was when I heard a whole new term that stuck with me. "Don't be a fun sucker," said my son. I volleyed back, "A fun sucker? What's a fun sucker?" I kind of knew what the answer was going to be. He said, "A person that sucks the fun out of things." I eventually got on that tube.

The lesson I learned, however, was that sometimes anyone can be a fun sucker. So you need to make sure that you do not behave that way when you are with your employees. Do not be a stuffed shirt. Loosen up a bit!

In every workplace culture, you will find examples of individuals who fit into one of these four quadrants of play. Our objective is to bring people along and move them toward the top right quadrant—the Player (initiator). Play has multiple meanings for us, and it can be used in so many ways within an innovative, modern organization.

- *Play to be productive:* Snowfly, a tech-based company, motivates employees using games and has reported a 95% approval rating[2] among users. Workers compete to earn tokens and prizes, and they love it.
- *Play to lead*: Playing at work develops a better leadership style, and games can even help you grow as a leader.

---

2 Christopher Null, Does Gaming at Work Improve Productivity, http://www.pcworld.com/article/155284/gamingatwork.html

According to Steffen Lofvall,[3] games are a great leadership tool because they accelerate learning while making it fun.

- *Play to unite*: Games and playing in the workplace unite teams, which results in a stronger collaborative environment. A team at Blue Ridge Bank[4] used a Lego Serious Play method to invite collaboration in uneasy teams. It was a resounding success.
- *Play to be innovative and curious*: With Pew Research reporting[5] that more than half of all adults are gamers, these fun sessions of play can inspire creativity and curiosity in otherwise disengaged minds.

The Study of Play: Maslow's Missing Need?

Play may just be the missing need that Maslow left off his hierarchy. It is the essential element that is lacking in workplaces across America—and indeed the world—right now.

I remember once, when I was presenting a training session on creativity at Disney Studios in Burbank, California, that I encountered a great example of play. There were these larger than life cartoon characters that were drawing whimsical things in the lobby of the building I was training in. The moment you stepped into their presence, you felt the fun, playful atmosphere. Interestingly, it attracted a lot of people—like a siren call for fun.

In many uncomfortable situations, humor allows you to accept an avenue of discussion. It influences how people think

---

[3] Susanne Garguilo, Play to Win: Work Games Can Give a Career Power Up, http://edition.cnn.com/2013/02/27/business/work-simulation-games-route-to-the-top/

[4] Blue Ridge Bank, Serious Banking, http://www.seriousplay.com/18045/BLUE%20RIDGE%20BANK

[5] Ross Smith, Communicate Hope: Using Games and Play to Improve Productivity, http://www.managementexchange.com/story/communicate-hope-using-games-and-play-improve-productivity-42projects

and behave by elevating their emotional and motivational states. That means humor can elevate your mood by creating a buffer against anything that is complex, mundane, or boring.

Humor is a major motivation booster,[6] and a motivated employee is an innovative and creative one. Momentum can be harnessed to improve performance by using play mechanics instead of traditional processes. You see, really great businesses do not focus on individual stars but on a system where everyone can shine if they do great work.

That means that what people need is more than what Maslow originally suggested. Along with his core physical and psychological needs (self-actualization, esteem, love, belonging, safety, food, etc.), Maslow should have added "play" as a method to facilitate work. Play actually integrates and promotes all other needs in his hierarchy, which makes it critically important.

Look at it this way. An employee could be creative, part of a great team, well fed, well rested, safe, and respected—but still not producing at their level of potential. By cutting out play, modern society has inadvertently caused stress levels to rise to levels people have never experienced before. No wonder there is so much ill health in the world right now!

By studying play and how it should be used in your workplace—or used as part of your unique leadership style—you can regain a powerful balance that will help your teams become highly successful no matter what they do.

The Changing Faces of Corporate Play

Play has never been a simple, basic thing—though it has evolved into simplistic distraction methods for children. To put it in context, I want to give you a rule of thumb to remember. The

---

[6] Dr Paul McGhee, Humor Helps Produce an Emotionally Intelligent Workplace, http://www.laughterremedy.com/article_pdfs/Emotional%20Intelligence.pdf

rule of thumb phrase was originally said to be derived from the belief that a man could beat his wife with a stick as long as it was no bigger than his thumb.

Of course, this is completely unproven and is likely an old fallacy or joke. It does make the phrase "rule of thumb" memorable, though, because of that fun story.

Play is, in fact, a process and not a place. When leaders think of business oriented functions like personal growth and development, skill building, and learning, the very last thing that enters their minds is play. Yet for a leader that understands the King Atys way, play can get you there quicker than just about any other process.

The American Psychological Association has conducted studies on how fun and features of fun—like humor and silliness—can rapidly improve learning. According to John Hopkins University,[7] being engaged and laughing at something is the best way to remember it.

Engaged thought is one of the most powerful assets you can develop as a leader, and the key to this lies in world class awareness—the kind you get from learning through play. I might even venture further than that and say that for leaders, play is the most powerful skill that they can learn to further their career and make them better leaders.

The question then becomes—*how do I become a more playful leader?* The rest of this book will walk you through it. It is first imperative that you understand the changing faces of corporate play. While back in King Atys' time play was an essential tool that saved his entire empire, these days it is approached with hostility and skepticism.

---

[7] Zak Stambor, How Laughing Leads to Learning, http://www.apa.org/monitor/jun06/learning.aspx

In the few companies where play has been instated as an essential process, these teams of people have thrived. But no one benefits more than The Playful Leader. As I mentioned earlier, it takes a strong leader to bring play back to the workplace and prove that it has a serious place there. I am not playing around!

The rule of thumb needs to be that all play needs to begin with the leader of an organization. It has to trickle down into every department so that it can perform its vital functions of reducing stress, enhancing performance, and improving self-development, creativity, and team work.

People play games in modern society to unwind, get exercise, de-stress, and let loose. Let's bring these vital functions back into the workplace—where you can benefit from them. It all begins with you as the first playful leader in your organization.

A Refreshing Model of Productive Play

Play is complex and multi-faceted, but The Play Matrix Model is not. Just when you believe it has worked on one crucial area of your company, it has moved on and fixed several other issues. When you invite productive play into your company, you are doing so much more than just "lightening things up" a little.

It reminds me of a fishing trip that I took with my son. One day, on the Skyline Drive, we were fishing along the stream that flowed into Electric Lake. As we were preparing our lures, my son turned to me and said, "Do you see the fish?" I could not see them—just the water streaming by. He was wearing glasses with polarized lenses that allowed him to see more than I could. The Playful Leader walks around with polarized lenses on and sees opportunities to engage in productive play.

Because of play, you become more aware of the people, processes, and places around you—and how they function. You begin to see things that you did not see before. And that is why play can do the most incredible things for your business—things that you cannot even see yet. The benefits are consistent and far reaching.

- The Play Matrix Model is a refreshingly simple and intuitive strategy that works to identify personality types and helps you integrate them into your new system.
- The old "hey kids, get off my lawn!" approach is not working in business anymore. People want to be happy where they work, how they work, and who they work for. In fact, a lot of the most in-demand talent is going to companies that have integrated play into their daily operations.
- The play and work model has been diametrically opposed. Right now, our leadership style may be unbalanced and only contain elements of serious work. Not only are we unbalanced, but there are daily opportunities for growth and far-reaching benefits that we have not even realized.
- The worst thing you can do is withhold play because you think that there is some risk involved. The real risk has always been running your company without any semblance of productive play in the workplace. Common symptoms include stressed, disillusioned, and burnt-out staff.
- Make use of play platforms! These communication tools are designed to leverage the creative efforts of employees by sharing tactics to elicit productive play. Take note of the word "productive" here. All play needs to have a purpose, be part of an overarching strategy, or be used to improve your employee performance.

The bottom line for you as a playful leader is that play pays. Happy workers spend 80%[8] of their time on work-related tasks,

---

[8] Having Fun at Works Pays Off, http://bvblog.baudville.com/post/2010/08/26/Having-Fun-at-Work-Pays-Off.aspx#.U3842PmSySo

and unhappy workers spend 40% of their time on work-related tasks. Clearly, a happy, playful team member is a hard-working business asset.

Keep those playful glasses on.

My simplified model of productive play looks like this:

SIMPLIFIED MODEL
- *SEE THE FUNNY*
- *IT'S OK TO PLAY*
- *BE PLAYFUL*
- *SCALE PLAY*

As leaders, it is important that we tune in to and "see the funny" around us. We must let ourselves and others know that "it's okay to play." Then simply "be playful" and, finally, "scale play" in your organization.

04

The Seesaw Effect (Play Structures)

"The true object of all human life is play. Earth is a task garden; heaven is a playground."

GILBERT K. CHESTERTON

Imagine strolling through a park along a gentle path. There, in the middle of a playground, is an empty seesaw (some call it a teeter totter). As you pass the structure, you think, "Man, I would really like to go for a ride." So you sit down. At first, you sit on the low end of the seesaw, and you wait. But you do not seem to be getting anywhere.

Then you look up and see the high side: yes, that is where you want to be! So you jump off and attempt to climb the high end...but it crashes down. Once again, you are on the low side, not having any fun. If you are motivated and clever enough, you can come up with many ways of getting you higher—sand bags and passersby.

Finding Play in the System

If you are lucky, you will meet a person—like you—who really wants to ride the seesaw. However, most people cannot be bothered, or they do not have the time. Those that might have been interested were too afraid. There you sit, alone on your seesaw.

This principle is directly related to play in the workplace. There are various play structures that you can institute at work, but ultimately, it is a big shift, and people are going to be confused by and wary of it. The seesaw effect explains the balancing act involved in instituting the playful culture in your organization.

Imagine your new playful culture as the center piece (or fulcrum) of the seesaw. The bottom, on the ground, is your results, and high on the other end is the amount of effort that you put in. On the other end, you need to initially put effort into play.

The Seesaw Effect

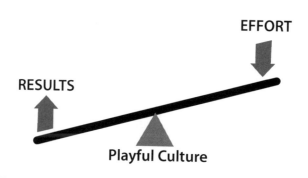

As you introduce a new organizational culture, there is a shift that begins to take place. The fulcrum moves, and the amount of effort is reduced. You are building a framework for others.

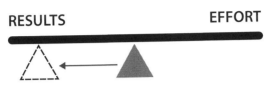

With a shift in culture the leadership effort can decrease and still achieve high levels of purposeful play.

Simply by moving this center piece to the true "center" of your seesaw, you can find that magic balance. With a shift in culture, the leadership effort can decrease while you still achieve high levels of purposeful play.

Knowing how to build great play structures will keep you mastering your results while leading your company into a new era of work–play balance. Both are achievable, but you have to begin by instituting The Playful Leader Matrix tactics.

- To find play in the system, you need to look for it. Where are people the unhappiest? Where are the most boring, mundane, and repetitive tasks? How can you improve these and make them more fun?

Lead Out With Permission to Play

The second step is to give people permission to play. I will dive deeper into permission in the next chapter. That means focusing on fun and formulating a business culture around your specific play structures. A play structure is a type of strategy that you will use to motivate people to engage in playful behavior.

- Solo play involves instituting structures where your employees can enjoy playing on their own. How can I make work playful in my own little playground?
- Pair play is getting two people involved in the same play. This begins with invitations to play (verbal and non-verbal) and the inclination to join play invitations extended by others.
- Team play involves building structures that promote team play environments, group fun, and shared experiences. These are great for teamwork and fostering a real sense of playful culture in your business.

When I teach people about the merits of play, I quickly realize that some people are resisting. Some people do not want to play. They fit into the most difficult play role, "the will not play" group. For all other segments—the cannots, wills, and dos—these people will become your core play teams. But do not give up on the "won'ts." Here are some great examples!

- Ryan is 34 and a computer programmer. He is also a resister, which means that he is a rampant fun sucker. He won't play, *but* he may be willing to learn how to play if taught and given permission.
- Olivia is 21 and an admin clerk. She is an observer, which means that she is a fun watcher and will not join in on the fun, *but* she will join in if invited or given permission to play.
- Wyatt is 48 and a project manager. He is a wisher, which means that he is a fun seeker and will join in when play if shown how (given permission or some tactics).
- Isabel is 26 and a creative art director. She is an initiator, which means that she is a natural player and does play, in a purposeful way.

While Isabel will be leading each activity—with Wyatt close on her heels—Wendy will watch from the sidelines as Ryan ignores everyone altogether. As The Playful Leader, you need to learn to identify these people in your company so that you can integrate them into your new system. The play structures that you institute will be modeled by and through them.

The most important thing here is that you give people permission to be playful by being playful yourself and building a culture of playfulness by creating "play opportunities" at work. Natural playgrounds, improvisation, and non-verbal play—these are all structures that you can create. The employees that enjoy them will take advantage of them.

Put Productive Play to Work

I was setting up for a training session in Seattle, Washington, when a participant walked in about 30 minutes early. I was the only person in the room. She looked around and then said, "Oh, it is going to be an interactive one." I could not tell if she was happy about that or sad. I thought "interactive one" was a good thing, but some people just do not want to be *interactive*.

The session went well, and afterwards, that same lady approached me. "I want to apologize," she said. I looked at her: "For what?" She told me how she arrived at the training session with a poor attitude and stuck in a bad mood. She thanked me for making the session playful and well worth her time. I guess sometimes you need to play up and out of your misery!

The third step in instituting your Playful Leader Matrix is to put productive play to work. You know that old adage *"Be the change that you want to see in the world"*? It applies here. Using clarity, brevity, and frequency, you will actively put that productive play to work in your company.

- Play at work needs to be clearly defined so that no one has to worry about getting into trouble.
- Play at work needs to be centered around brevity; in other words, it has to be brief and concise in order to re-motivate quickly so that people can not only continue to work but work harder.
- Play at work needs to be frequent, which means that it has to happen often, or a few times during your average work day.

Think about play like it is a game. There are players, coaches, spectators, and cheerleaders. There are also benchwarmers! People will assume their natural roles, and everyone will have a good time (while being productive). However, there does not need to be benchwarmers, because everyone can play.

It will be your job to set the stage for this play, which means creating ongoing structures. There may be some specific areas within your company where productive play is not only allowed but enthusiastically encouraged.

Ideally, you will want to institute structured play and random play models so that you can also take advantage of the naturally fun "spontaneity" of play. A company that leaves bouncing balls lying around, for example, will encourage employees to use them whenever they are feeling stressed or need a break. And yet it does not always require a ball to play. It is a state of mind. It is a state of play.

Cadence of play is also something to consider, and it refers to patterns and rhythms that promote fun and activity. A great example is Lego[9] and how building a structure in a team can help each member get to know each other and develop bonds of friendship beyond what they are doing.

---

9   Mike Donachie, The Lego Guys Will Help You Build Your Company's Team, Brick by Brick, http://metronews.ca/news/london/1013301/the-lego-guys-will-help-build-your-companys-team-brick-by-brick/

Push the Play Boundaries

I was invited to speak to a group of managers that was with Lucky Brand Jeans in Los Angeles. I decided it would be fun to wear a pair of their jeans to the event. I loaded the car with my wife and my daughter and her husband and asked them to help me buy these $100.00 jeans. I have always been a bit of a Levi's guy, so I needed help because I was not used to spending that kind of money on jeans.

We drove to the outlet mall in Park City, and shortly afterwards, I had my first pair of designer jeans. I arrived at the JW Marriot LA Live in Los Angeles and walked down the hall towards the conference room. There I noticed an attractive young lady looking at me. I was sure that she was with Lucky Brands and that she had noticed I was wearing "her" jeans.

I was introduced as the speaker and started to do my thing. I announced that I was sporting my new Lucky Brand jeans and that they have changed my life. Women were finally starting to notice me! Then I picked the girl out of the audience and asked her to stand. "Were you looking at me in the hallway?" I asked. She nodded. "And what, may I ask, were you looking at?" She responded, "Your jeans!" The audience laughed.

This was a classic playground moment. These "moments" happen all the time in your daily work life. People just let them roll by. But they are always chances to connect, joke around, and lighten everyone's load. You need to be willing to initiate playground moments in your life. That also means accepting play invitations when they are extended to you.

PLAY

Watch for opportunities to accelerate play by extending an invitation to join in the fun (come on in, the water is warm). Flying on a smaller regional jet to Los Angeles with limited overhead space, the US Airways employee took my roller bag to check and said, "I'll make sure this gets to Denver," while maintaining an expressionless face. Then a smile erupted. That was an invitation to play. Be prepared to initiate and join playground moments.

Extend Play Boundaries
(invite, initiate, include, expand)

Then watch for opportunities to extend play or scale play. If this airline employee were brave, he could have hollered down the jetway for all to hear something like, "You can pick up your roller bags in Denver; we'll be arriving at gate B21!"

Too few people have fun at work. Like anything fun, it requires effort and a desire to bring something to life. Never underestimate the desire of a co-worker to have some fun. They will bring the effort if you bring the permission.

Playground Analogy (Sandbox, Seesaw, Slide, Swing)

Each phase of The Playful Leader philosophy is represented by a playground structure. This makes it fun to learn and easier to remember for new playful leaders.

- The seesaw shows you how things need to be balanced, so you have to actively look for play in your systems. You need to balance your leadership load with the right amount of effort so that you can promote a playful culture in the workplace.
- The swing shows you that you need to shift your culture so that your leadership effort can decrease and you can achieve a higher level of purposeful play. When you give your employees permission to play, many of them will embrace the opportunity.
- The slide represents your need to put productive play to work in your company. You cannot be too serious or play will be ineffective. You cannot be too frivolous or play will still be ineffective. You must aim for the top of the slide at the height of the curve so that play can be truly effective—using clarity, brevity, and frequency.

- The sandbox shows you how you should always push or extend the boundaries of play by inviting people to play, initiating play, and including others in your play. Creating playground moments and *being* a real playful leader will help.

Your company is like a large playground. When you implement these models, it will be like you are building real-world playground structures into your business. At each phase, your employees will begin to embrace the opportunities that you offer them—first the players, then the fun seekers, then the fun watchers, and finally, the fun suckers.

- They will seesaw their way to play by noticing how you have been changing the culture in your business.
- They will swing across to your side of thinking when they know that they have been given clear rules and permission to play.
- They will slide right into productive play routines as long as they know exactly what they can do, for how long, and how often.
- Finally, they will become part of your sandbox, where playground moments are embraced and everyone in your company invites, initiates, and includes others in their daily productive play opportunities.

When you use The Playful Leader Matrix and these structured tactics, it becomes easier to identify and facilitate play opportunities in your workplace. Remember, you have to live the culture and consistently let your employees know that it is okay for them to play.

The Seesaw Effect (Play Structures)

Your Fear of Fun Is Holding You Back

I sometimes hear the term "forced fun." Perhaps, in some cases, you should not tell people that they are about to have fun.

For many employees, the idea of having fun at work is so foreign that they cannot comprehend it. But there are many reasons why your employees might resist your new play culture:

- They outright reject play and have no desire to play at work. These people love to work, and they would never dream of doing anything like "having fun" on the job.
- They do not know how. Because of years of being told that play at work is wrong, many people will have no concept of what play is, how it is done, or what the rules might be for enjoying themselves at work.
- They do not have permission. Resistance is often a direct result of employees not having permission to play. They fear for their jobs and do not want to upset the equilibrium by doing anything new.

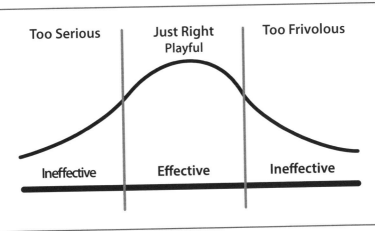

The Play Curve is all about balance—reaching the right peak in your company with just rhe right amount of playfulness for everyone to enjoy. If your company is too serious, or too frivolous, your play models are going to work against productivity and the benefit of your employees.

I like to think of it like the Goldilocks and the three bears story. This is the analogy you should keep in mind when adjusting to the play curve. Every brand will need to find the right balance to keep everyone happy and benefitting from "just the right" amount of productive play.

The same can be said for you, The Playful Leader. Leaders might still have bosses, and all of these resistant traits may apply to you as well. Use this approach to make incremental improvements in your current performance—and in the performance of your employees—and soon bosses everywhere will be embracing the concept.

There are three things that you need to focus on during implementation:

1. *Your mindset:* This involves how you think it is important and why you think it is important. You need to think with playful excitement so that you can show others what it is like.
2. *Your skillset:* How you implement fun and play into your normal work day will set the tone for your leadership style and how your teams perform or improve their skills.
3. *Your toolset:* These are the tools that you are going to use to help others interpret your play culture, and play during their average day will be important.

To become The Playful Leader, you have to realize that you are going to encounter resistance. Sometimes you will be able to change that person's mind, other times not. Everyone is different, especially in this age of "what the boss says goes.'" Entire companies are built around what the owners want instead of what is good for the people and company.

Play Orientation: The History and Rules

Work is instrumental in our lives. What is your career? Where do you work? What do you do? How much do you earn? The list goes on. So when you step into your company and attempt to reorient your workforce on play and what it can do for everyone, you will need to set some very strict rules.

- *Physical rules of play*: Establish physical rules of play that include what can be done and done to who—and clearly state how employees may or may not engage each other in pranks and general frivolous fun.
- *Verbal rules of play*: Establish verbal rules that include what can be said, how and what should not be said to keep everyone happy, and toeing the line.
- *Emotional rules of play*: Establish rules for emotional enjoyment that include things like letting others win, leaving good things for each other to find (not just pranks), and supporting each other with fun in times of need.
- *Mental rules of play*: Establish rules for mental enjoyment. Keep things happy, positive, and geared towards sharing a common experience.

For one thing, fun is not always play—and play is not always fun. It depends on context, whom you are with, and what you are doing. It also depends on past experiences. As a playful leader, it will be your job to monitor your employees and make sure that everyone is integrated and enjoying the new moments of play at work.

Sometimes playing by the rules takes on a literal meaning and becomes a new company motto for you and your team. Based on your past models built, that will determine how to roll out your new future.

It always helps if you have a team of people on your side to begin with, so work on that. They will prove that the models will require team support and a healthy load of fun.

Work, Lead, and Sell: What Play Does Best

Peter Drucker once said, "Culture eats strategy for lunch." He is right on. When you build a business that is based on a playful culture, it restructures everything—from the way people think to how they work and engage with each other. You need to figure out how to let everyone play within the context of what they do for a living.

What play does for your employees is give them a reason to work hard. It gives you a reason to lead well. It gives your marketing department a reason to sell tons of products. Play becomes the reason people want to go to work because their jobs become fun. And fun jobs are desirable jobs that attract the best talent.

While there is always a potential cost for fun, it pales in comparison to how people are made to function right now—with no happiness, play, or fun during their entire work day.

Employees that are creative, smart, and curious are also often restless. They need new challenges and interesting things happening around them. When you institute play at work, it gives these people an instant outlet. Sometimes all it takes is a fifteen-minute break to keep someone working double time for the next four hours.

And that is perhaps what play does best of all. It allows people to be themselves at work, gives them the freedom to think and grow, and brings similar minds together. Without play, some people would never have met others from different departments and created something new. You have to believe in the systems and culture that you build.

Serve, Teach, Innovate: Improving With Play

The reason why play has grown is because it fuels the right kind of business culture. Humor really does energize people and helps them be creative, friendly, and sharp in the workplace. You could even argue that positive relationships between workplace fun and job satisfaction will only happen if the individual involved has a positive attitude towards fun.

That is why you need to consider improving the culture of play while concurrently teaching your employees to become ambassadors for your system. Everyone in your company has the ability to improve with play; they just need some direction.

- *Serve*: As The Playful Leader, you need to serve those around you and teach others to do the same. People can only have fun if everyone is being accommodating and unselfish and thinking of others first.
- *Teach*: You need to educate your teams on how to advocate your culture of fun in the workplace so that they can show others how to play in the right context. That way you will spread the message and the good results.
- *Innovate*: Part of having fun and playing at work involves innovation, creation, and putting something together that is outside the box. Educate your employees about this, and show them how play can help innovation get off the ground.
- *Love*: Be a loving leader. Love what you do. Love your employees and customers, and let it show. Love being a part of your organization. Love is a powerful emotion.

The essence of play is a new way of thinking, designing, and implementing solutions. It is really a major cultural shift, where work–life balance now becomes work–play balance. Life is already happening, and it is a part of work and play!

Games, challenges, and competitions have been permanent fixtures in human society. It is about time they made a strong return to the working arena. You will need to apply a layered approach, where focus and pace of adoption will differ by industry or individual company dynamics. Each company (and individual) has its own ideas on what play means.

Some may say a finance company may find that play only works on a very limited, restricted basis—purely because of where they are and what they do. I do not believe this. On the other hand, a tech start-up can revel in creativity and play—with their own play rooms, models, and structures that will keep their employees moving, engaged, and having a great time. We can all be equal opportunity players.

- Encourage spontaneity on the job; it is central to fun. Do not allow restraint to kill your employees' capacity for doing something different.
- Fun is multi-dimensional; there can be formal fun activities, fun co-worker interactions (joke time at the water cooler), or fun workplace responsibilities. Some formal forms of fun include work theme days, parties, picnics, and outings.
- Play naturally inspires more play, so once you get going, the culture will be easy to adopt. Then you need to continue to encourage productive play.

The Fun Theory or Piano Stairs

Have you ever heard of the fun theory? This is a theory that follows the premise that making something fun is the easiest way to change a person's behavior for the better. Think about that for a second and really consider how powerful this concept can be!

In Odenplan in Stockholm, the fun theory was applied to some stairs in order to get people to take them instead of the escalator. The escalator was great, but exercise is a critical part of health. In reality, the stairs make you feel better because they give you exercise and fresh endorphins. But everyone chose to use the escalator because they were tired and unmotivated.

When the fun theory was applied, the challenge became to get more people to take the stairs! The tactic that they used was simple. They turned the regular staircase into a piano staircase. The stairs made sounds, just like the keys on a piano. This basic change resulted in 66%[10] more people choosing to take the stairs. Amazing!

This is solid proof that the fun theory works like a bomb. People could see that the piano keys were just stairs, but because it looked like fun, the decision was easy. Apply this theory to work, and you have an amazing tool on your side.

It also pays to play with the moment. Being present allows you to be spontaneous. Too many employees are withdrawn and live in the future or in the past.

- *Play is an event at level one*: This means that in the beginning, everyone will treat your play as a special event.
- *Play is a process at level two*: Once they have become used to these events, play begins to become more like a process—or something that needs to be carried out for certain outcomes to be achieved.

---

[10] The Piano Stairs of Fun Theory – Short Run Fun and Not a Nudge, http://www.inudgeyou.com/the-piano-stairs-of-fun-theory-short-run-fun-and-not-a-nudge/

- *Play is a system at level three*: Finally, when you reach level three, play becomes a system integrated into your company just like any other. This is when play has been fully recognized and ratified into a cultural existence.

It pays to play because it affects your business on multiple levels. It makes you a more efficient leader. It makes your employees more productive and better connected to each other, which improves company morale and culture. It increases revenues, reduces dissatisfaction, and opens up new creative possibilities that did not exist before.

Three Success Stories of Fun-Loving Companies

When Volkswagen began their new campaign on the fun theory, they tested it by setting up lots of cameras in public places.[11] In one area, they set up a bottle arcade, or a fun way of disposing of bottles in an area where this was not done as much as it could have been.

The video is further proof that the fun theory works. People organically look for ways to have fun in their day-to-day lives. Because they are prevented from having fun at work, they need to get their fun from somewhere else. VW certainly hit the mark with these campaigns, proving that a spirit of fun can have a greater impact than people think.

Then there are the ever popular Google slides. These are a critical part of their fun-loving business culture, and they help keep very intelligent, highly stressed employees relaxed and having fun. Google also has fireman poles and cattle walkways, all important parts of the play culture for the most powerful company in the world today.

---

[11] The Fun Theory: Volkswagen Masters the Viral Video, http://mashable.com/2009/10/11/the-fun-theory/

The Seesaw Effect (Play Structures)

A closer look at Google play culture reveals even more than the "average" slides and poles. Nap rooms,[12] wall art, special food rooms, employee character drawings that get color after a year, sports scoreboards, Star Trek rooms, and basketball nets are not uncommon there.

So where is the proof that all of this wacky culture works? You only have to look at Google's growing numbers, revenue, and reach to see that. Google has also filed more patents recently than almost any other company in the world, and they have been instrumental in the advancement of search technology, wearable technology, and other future tech.

Interestingly enough, Best Buy, the huge publicly-traded electronics company, has also had great success establishing a culture of play with their employees. At their break room in Union Square in Manhattan, you will find videogames, foosball tables, and giant TVs, where after hours, they host video competitions and movie events.

Every year, the store sends 2000 supervisors to Phoenix to test a bunch of new gaming consoles and gadgets for the holidays. Back at corporate headquarters, it is not as stuffed shirt as you would think. They have a "results only" work environment, which means that you can make your own hours as long as the work gets done.

For many similar stores in the Best Buy niche, things are not going so well. But Best Buy is fast recovering, and they have reported a profit in 2013. Clearly, if you want to make your staff happy and see your business do better than previous years, fun may be the remedy.

---

12   This Google Office Has a Real Fireman's Pole, Slide, Cattle Walkway and More, http://venturebeat.com/2013/05/08/this-google-office-has-a-real-firemans-pole-slide-cattle-walkway-and-more-gallery/

PLAY

These many play rituals, formulas, and structures encourage the people that work in these companies to connect so that they become loyal to their brands and to their co-workers. *Companies that have fun together, stay together!*

05

Permission to Play Your Best Hand

> "You can discover more about a person in an hour of play than in a year of conversation."
>
> PLATO

Now that you are perfectly oriented in the playground models and structures that you could use to implement your play culture, the next step is to take a closer look at how you are going to behave as The Playful Leader controlling your new culture.

As I started to do research for this book, it hit me. This is a book about leadership. Yes, we are all leaders with or without a title, but so much of productive play will stem from management. Leaders must demonstrate the productive play attributes. Leaders must give people permission to play. They must know it is okay to play and that this productive play will lead to increased performance.

You need to give yourself personal permission to have fun in a productive way. You also need to make sure that your supervisor has given you the same permission, if possible. It may be a risky proposition for management, but it brings people together. You should always be willing to push the boundaries of play for yourself and others.

There will be rules for play just like there are rules for work. Rules give people security and permission. But you, as the leader, need to get into the habit of creating (and noticing) these playground moments and accepting the invitation to engage playfully with your staff.

Sometimes even the most successful play-oriented leaders find it hard to make the change. Ultimately, however, becoming a playground architect is incredibly rewarding, and it will take your teams to renewed innovation, better attitudes, and stronger bonds.

Becoming a Playground Architect

There is no better way to show others that you are human and approachable than self-deprecating humor. Can you laugh at yourself? Are you comfortable in your own skin? These are marks of a person that can use self-deprecation to connect with others.

Cecily Cooper, an associate professor at the University of Miami School of Business, says that "If you're in a position of power, self-deprecating humor is very safe and makes others more inclined to like you by reducing the power distance that exists."

I totally agree with that, having used self-deprecating humor many times myself to disarm my audiences and connect with them emotionally.

New research shows that great leaders tend to be funny in a particular way. There are three anecdotes that correspond to three different humor styles: group-deprecating, aggressive, and self-deprecating. Project managers that use self-deprecating humor test high for transformational leadership, defined by motivational qualities like trust and likability.

"Everyone makes mistakes," said Colette Hoption,[13] a management professor at Seattle University. "Admitting them frankly can help build solid relationships with your team."

The three different types of humor can be expressed like this:

1. *Group-deprecating:* "I am impressed John transferred despite knowing all about us."
2. *Aggressive:* "I am impressed John transferred despite knowing all about you."
3. *Self-deprecating:* "I am impressed John transferred despite knowing all about me."

Studies have been done on self-deprecating humor, and it can break down barriers and help you connect with your teams. The "it's not you, it's me" line of jokes always tend to work in a crowd of employees. However, they can also backfire and exacerbate differences between employees and their leaders.

The findings of the study[14] concluded that self-deprecating humor, when used correctly, can be a great tool to even out the power tensions in working relationships. Because of the new generations coming into the workplace—with new communication skills and challenges—the gap has grown even larger. To connect, these power dynamics must work for you.

To become a playground architect, you need to be well versed in the ways of different types of humor. For example, the Nerf

---

13   Eric Markowitz, Brilliant Leaders Use This Type of Humor (Hint: Think Woody Allen), http://www.inc.com/magazine/201306/eric-markowitz/humor-self-deprecation-leaders.html

14   Colette Hoption, "It's Not You, It's Me": Transformational Leadership and Self-Deprecating Humor, http://www.emeraldinsight.com/journals.htm?articleid=17076800

gun used in Zappos' offices is a metaphor for openness. Anyone, at any time, can grab the gun and shoot at someone else.

Play needs to be modeled by management first. That means that you have to lead the "play" charge for your employees. Many playful leaders get almost no training, no support, and no encouragement at all to create an atmosphere of fun at work. The current model was pervasive at every level of most organizations, so first-line supervisors had no models to imitate.

A classical mindset and a narrow set of technically oriented skills made it unsurprising that workplaces were historically devoid of laughter, spontaneity, light-heartedness, and enjoyment. But this is what you need to bring back—by your own behavior, the way that you train your management teams, and how they pass on the actions to their employees.

One trait that consistently ranks high among the most admired leaders is that they are confident enough to poke fun at themselves. Smart leaders always recognize that they are a potential punch line and a great way to break down barriers.

The Virtues of Curiosity and Exploration

Two of the most important virtues to pass on to your teams are curiosity and exploration. These traits have to be practiced in your own leadership style. Sometimes this means infiltrating play principles behind enemy lines for those "stay off my lawn" types that have made it clear that they do not want to play.

You can role play as a travel guide, teaching your teams that the process of play is more important than the purpose. They should not take themselves seriously, and you need to give them explicit permission to have fun in a variety of ways. Many of your team members will only need permission to play; they do not need to be taught how.

These individuals are naturally curious and explorative,

though these traits have been horribly suppressed by the play-devoid system. You need to introduce fun into your work culture one element at a time. Together, your teams will discover a sense of purpose with the play that you institute. I have seen it happen time and time again.

When you bring your own sense of play in the form of curiosity and exploration, you teach others what play ethic is all about. You will find many managers that cannot play are merely expressing their insecurity about losing control.

You need to come up with innovative ways to show your customers, bosses, and employees that it is okay to indulge in productive play. When an office is free and secure enough to play without judgment, the people there take more creative risks that pay off. Only you have the power to decide whether or not you are going to be a roadblock or a catalyst for play.

Company leaders need to be more human. Get your leaders to share personal details about themselves for everyone to enjoy. What was their favorite band growing up? What was their most embarrassing moment? Put it on the company blog or the newsletter. Allow people to get to know each other by being naturally curious and explorative.

- Managerial support for fun begins with the CEO. At the company ice cream social, the CEO should be there with everyone else, chatting to employees and supervisors. It sends the right message—that fun is encouraged—because play flows from the top down and through all the layers.
- Some employers encourage gaming on the job. Monterey Bay Area Paramedics[15] work long shifts overnight, so management encourages them to play casual games like Bejeweled on their PDAs to prevent sleep from kicking in.

---

15   Ian Wylie, More Play, More Work, http://www.theguardian.com/money/blog/2009/jan/07/playing-games-at-work

Imaginative and Solo Play: What You Need to Know

You cannot, as The Playful Leader, expect all forms of play to succeed. Sometimes they will fail. In some games, there are losers as well as winners. That means that there will be people that do not want to take part, because they might not win.

This is why you need to create an introductory statement about the magic that happens when we play. You will get more done. You will make that sale. You will become more influential. Investing in play—whether it is your time, desire, ideas, or energy—always pays off. Once you implement a play strategy, you will see the results.

Aside from that, research has shown that managers who have taught themselves to be funnier are more effective communicators, better sales people, have more engaged employees, earn a lot more than their peers, and are much thinner. Okay, maybe not the last one. But playfulness is power when strategy is applied.

Controlling Your Fun Time!

Control, as I mentioned earlier, is a double-sided ax that can cut down your efforts at fun and play if you are not careful. People need to be handed a "hall pass" for play, with the knowledge that there will be no criticism or backlash if they embrace the opportunity.

Once you have convinced yourself that making work fun is not only enjoyable but that it boosts performance and improves so many other areas, you will need to introduce elements of fun into your work setting. Every company is different. You will have your own unique considerations and influences on what will work and what will not work.

Whatever approach you choose to adopt, you need to sustain and maintain your standards of competence and professionalism, even when you are having fun.

- ***Play environments***: You will construct certain play environments that offer your employees the opportunity to steal a moment of fun. Some great examples are the slides at Google or the Nerf guns that line the halls of Zappos.
- ***Dedicated play times***: Focus on solo play, pair play, and group play, and see where you get the best results by measuring the productivity boost and other metrics involved.
- ***Spontaneous play***: Integrate play into normal work experiences, like meetings and conferences. Create an environment for play, but nothing overt. Your surroundings should simply suggest that play is all right so that anyone can if they want to.

Come up with a play manifesto with your teams so that everyone can be involved in the process and can help make the rules. Remember that mandatory fun can strip people of their ability to have fun, which will lead to an inauthentic workplace.

Having fun at work is not about hosting fun events. It is an intentional feeling or culture that runs deep into your organization from the top down. You should challenge your leaders to reinvent themselves, others, and the business at large.

As long as you, as the driving force, do not become a play dictator, then you will be fine. Concede that fun has different meanings for everyone and that a few people even consider "work" to be fun. Allow people their freedom, but be the Pied Piper that guides them to better ways to play. Embrace the risks, and tolerate the occasional failures.

Nurturing a Culture of Play in Business

You cannot control play, but you can facilitate it and set rules about when play is all right. Context, education, and involving your workforce is important so that everyone fully understands what it is you are doing as well as why and how.

- As information about health, coping, and productivity reaches top management, we will see more elements of fun being integrated into the workplace.
- Remember, fun is permission based and filters from the top down. People emulate what they see their superiors do. Always maintain control, but do it through your own actions.
- Things as small as word choices can impact how employees interpret your new play mandate, so make sure that everything is done in context. Build your very own vocabulary for work-based play.
- Every play experience becomes a part of your brand story and culture. These can be shared with your customers and employees to make new connections and stronger bonds as the company grows.

Your new culture of play needs to emerge organically. You only have to guide it by following the advice that I have given you. Using humor and different forms of play—and taking different types of people into account—you should be able to get everyone excited about this company shift towards a more fun (and productive) workplace.

- Establish play rules along with your top management, and get your employees involved. They need to see the potential dangers and offer solutions so that everyone stays professional.

- Your job will be to monitor the fun and make sure that all of your established rules are being followed.

Keep in mind that while play can happen at work and fun can be had at work, it does not change the basic facts. All employees get paid to do a job, and that job must be done. They will always be afraid of overstepping the mark and getting fired. That is why your leadership team needs to blaze the fun trail.

Meaningful and successful work–life balance can only be achieved once fun exists in the workplace. Creating a more fun environment,[16] where rules can be stretched, is all about building a new culture from the ground up.

The Fun Factor: Apply Liberally

Applying these cultural changes liberally will pull your company out of the boring stage of business and transform it into a garden party. Fun can be had in the most exciting ways while still maintaining professionalism and work ethic.

- *Verbal humor*: Something that is said, stated, or uttered [17]
- *Non-verbal humor*: Something that is performed, done, or experienced

Amusement is the lead in for humor, and where there is amusement and humor, there will always be fun and opportunities for play. Applying these verbal and non-verbal forms of humor in the workplace should go a long way in redesigning your business culture.

---

16   Tracy Spielberger, All Work and No Play? There's a Better Way, http://www.playworks.org/blog/all-work-and-no-play-there%E2%80%99s-better-way

17   Lisa Goldstein Graham, What Is It Like to Be Funny? The Spontaneous Humor Producer's Subjective Experience, https://etd.ohiolink.edu/rws_etd/document/get/antioch1275056868/inline

As a fun experiment, I would urge you to test the "fun theory" for yourself to see what a huge impact it has on the people in your workplace.

Clearly, the fun factor is an issue that needs to be addressed in your working environment as soon as possible. I strongly suggest you keep track of the processes, plans, and strategies that you use to implement this new business culture in your company.

Seek permission then share permission and form a team that will help you monitor and measure the impact of the many play structures that you will implement. Once your top level management sees the change, they will become part of your new system.

06

Discovering Your Company Playground

> "This is the real secret of life—to be completely engaged with what you are doing in the here and now. And instead of calling it work, realize it is play."
>
> ALAN WILSON WATTS

Does your company have a history of play? Discovering your company playground is no easy task. You need to begin with isolated cases and characters and work your way up to allow for a playful culture to emerge with a little help from you.

Right now there are many people inside your company that would jump at the chance to help you institute these new changes in your organization. Together, you will be able to outline and analyze how your company has dealt with play in the past.

Converting Your Playground into a Powerhouse

Playground moments are powerful, and when they are shared and become the "norm" in your company, they turn your business into a productive powerhouse of play. I am not talking about disorganized chaos, but what I am talking about is structured play spaces, experimentation, and a measurable return on your play investment.

Remember the fun theory I spoke about in the previous chapter? I will often show my people these short viral "Fun Theory" videos to show them how fun changes people's behaviors—just like the engineers did when they changed those stairs to piano keys that played notes as people walked across them. These "fun alternatives" are very powerful.

When you put real time into discovering your company's playground, not only will your employees have more fun but you will gain a competitive advantage[18] over other brands. There might be some resistance to play in your productivity-obsessed business culture, but this will change as it becomes an essential part of your employees' days (and the productivity will increase).

In a recent JWT Intelligence report, 9 out of 10 adults stated that play should not only be a part of children's lives but adult's lives too. That said, half of all respondents said they do not have time for play just for fun's sake. Focus on your company playground, which includes a physical location and a state of mind.

- Determine the play potential for your supervisors, peers, and others within your organization. What is your personal play potential?
- Play potential is made out of understanding, awareness,

---

18   Nick Ayala, July Trend Report Examines "Play as a Competitive Advantage," http://www.jwtintelligence.com/2012/07/july-trend-report-examines-play-competitive-advantage/#axzz32yx5Hepg

attitude, desire, and effort. All of these need to be checked before a play culture can emerge.

My office is a playground, designed specifically to ignite imaginations and encourage employees to interact—because this is when great ideas happen. Fun in the workplace is a key mechanism for enhancing organizational effectiveness.

There is a modern workplace fun movement happening, so you need to encourage your managers to develop corporate cultures that promote play, fun, and more humor. You have the capacity to learn from the mistakes you make. The good news is that you will learn a lot in the beginning of the play process.

Setting the Boundaries of Play

I love boundaries. I particularly love the silence that accompanies them because it gives me a chance to change the way people feel about them. Play, like anything else, has boundaries. Steve Cody, co-founder and managing partner of Peppercomm, lets his employees take stand-up comedy classes.

Then he lets them perform in an actual New York nightclub with all their co-workers watching. Employees find the experience terrifying and bonding[19]—and it has become a core feature of their business culture. In this way, you have to understand how important it is that each and every employee understands and embraces your company's philosophies.

Play can be a huge metaphor for the people in your business. Taking things from ho-hum to ah-mazing needs to be a big goal for you. Every company's mission statement should say something about fun as a core value. Culture really does eat strategy for lunch. When people live happy and fulfilled lives, they are free to do the impossible and the incredible!

---

19 Funny, They Don't Look Like Comedians, http://www.peppercomm.com/news/press-release/funny-they-dont-look-like-comedians

In this way, you are setting boundaries while also setting people free. Seizing the opportunity to play in order to accelerate productivity is key to any modern business, where mundane tasks and daily slogging forces people to float in a never-ending pool of boring.

To experience this positive impact on productivity, quality, engagement, and retention, fun needs to be ingrained in the *work*, not only in the special occasions and events that are completely separate from work. A survey by the Society for Human Resource Management[20] discovered that more than three quarters of their respondents believe that companies that promote fun during work are more effective than companies that do not.

A few daring organizations have made fun their primary value—and it has resulted in positive energy for their staff, which makes for happier customers in the long run. The best characteristics of a fun workplace are happiness, light-heartedness, humor, cheerfulness, and amusement. These are gaining in value for businesses all over the country.

- It can be hard to know where to draw the line with colleagues and bosses in the workplace when fun is involved. It is best to "feel" how people respond to each other and to document boundaries as they arise.
- Alternatively, you can appoint a play team to collect survey results and responses from your employees so that you can design boundaries around what they feel most comfortable with.
- "Play by the rules" can become your play manifesto or charter for defining what kind of play is acceptable and

---

[20] SHRM, Fun Work Environment Survey, http://www.shrm.org/Research/SurveyFindings/Documents/SHRM%20Fun%20Work%20Environment%20Survey.pdf

where the limits are for employees. This will help create good guidelines for productive play.

As you implement your play culture, natural boundaries will arise. Make sure that you are aware of them, and inform your employees about any new rules. Just make sure that you do it in a fun way to keep the momentum going.

The Dimensions of Quality Play

"How important is quality play at work anyway?" you might ask. Year after year, the Great Place to Work Institute finds that companies on the Fortune 100 "best companies" lists score incredibly high when asked "Is this a fun place to work?" Clearly, success these days directly correlates to how much fun people are able to have at work.

There are many dimensions involved in quality play. Play is quite like an onion in that there are many layers that need to be built to form a decent play culture. And it sometimes makes managers cry. Here are some dimensions you may want to consider:

- Humor as a dimension of play has been used to express superiority one has over others, which dates back to Plato. In the context of the organization, this concept reinforces the need for structure, control, and conformity to the laws, rules, regulations, and procedures of the company. Play facilitates control!
- Design is part science, part art. It requires a balanced blend of play mechanics and a deliberate approach to defining when conditions are right for certain personality types. Poorly conceived initiatives will likely result in chaos.
- Whether cultivated or not, every business has a character of its own that is defined by committing to the mission,

vision, and core values of the organization. Once the culture is established, every single decision is made through that lens. The lens is the DNA of the company. I want to find the DNA of the funny bone.

Once you have gone through your initial testing phase and have discovered that fun makes work more enjoyable, boosts performance on multiple levels, and improves quality of service despite ever-increasing demands on employees, you need to introduce more fun into your work setting. How do you do that?

- **Understanding**: When your employees understand what play at work means, what it aims to achieve, and what the reasons are for its presence, they will embrace it.
- **Awareness**: When your employees are aware of a playful culture, they will embrace it more often. That means setting up models, structures, and opportunities for play.
- **Attitude**: Your employees need to have the right attitude towards play; therefore you need to work on adjusting how they feel about it so that people can feel at ease.
- **Desire**: All of your employees love to play. But they need to have a real desire to play at work—with colleagues—and this may need some support and encouragement.
- **Effort**: Everyone needs to put in some effort and invest in play. Playing and having fun is not a passive experience, so look for ways to get everyone involved—even the quiet ones!

Learning to Ask

After a long, hard day at the office, Archimedes went home. Man, was he tired. Deciding to take a long hot bath, Archimedes slipped into the tub and immersed himself in water. Suddenly, something hit him like a ton of bricks. The water rose. In Archimedes' mind, the volume of the immersed object was equal to the volume of the displaced water. It was a Eureka moment that came because his mind was open to the task—even though his body was off the clock.

Alice Flaherty is a renowned neuroscientist,[21] and she researched how dopamine is directly linked to creativity—which happens to be significantly influenced by "feel good" events like taking a bath or becoming distracted in some way. A relaxed state of mind is critical for creative insight.

Implementing fun in the workplace does not mean being silly or causing chaos in the office hallways. It is more about creating a relaxed, positive environment, where people can enjoy their work and these "inspired" moments can naturally happen. To get to that point, as I have mentioned previously, requires many layers of permission.

When employees are allowed to make their own mistakes, it diffuses fear of failure and creates a positive and supportive learning environment. Sponsor frequent contests that prompt employee engagement and teamwork. Host a worst tie contest or the ugliest mug in the office award. These are small methods of granting permission to have fun.

Before you move ahead with your play plans, it is important to make sure that your company will adjust their corporate culture for you. Sometimes you can get mixed messages about it. These mixed responses will keep people boxed in and your play culture boxed out.

Host a meeting with your top brass and discuss the many different types of play instruments you plan on marching into

---

21 Leo Wildrich, Why We Have Our Best Ideas in the Shower: The Science of Creativity, http://blog.bufferapp.com/why-we-have-our-best-ideas-in-the-shower-the-science-of-creativity

the business. Get them to sing along to the same tune as you, using as many positive data sources and slides as you can.

There are also deficient skills for facilitating fun at work, which could prevent people from adopting the new culture. A seminar leader may prompt play in a manager, but they may not know how to play themselves.

Like Archimedes in that hot tub, developing a culture of play will make everyone a little more open and therefore a lot more likely to have good ideas and solve critical problems. Your environment needs to be relaxed and stimulating, and a culture of collaboration should be promoted. The more people communicate, the more blind spots they see.

This is why when a manager is stuck on a problem, they will host a meeting. Their team may not be able to come up with a solution, but the chatting and brainstorming may trigger a solution in the manager's brain if fun is involved.

Leaders like you must learn to create an organizational culture where others apply innovative thinking to solve problems and develop new products or services. Growing a culture of innovation is not about hiring creative people. It is about giving your overall workforce permission to play, create, and innovate during work hours.

The Trust-to-Play Model in Business

As a general rule, I frequently ask leaders, "What does it feel like to work here?" The answer to that question is a very clear insight into business culture because the way people feel determines how they eventually behave. Your company playground is heavily contingent on your ability to institute the right culture adjustments from day one.

R. Buckminster Fuller once said, "You cannot change people. If you change the environment that the people are in, they will change."[22] That is why your models need to be built around trust. This is the single most profound element that will influence the success of your freshly adjusted business culture.

When you trust people to play[23] and to follow your play rules, they will do it all on their own. Enforce these rules too much, and people will stop playing. Neglect to enforce them at all, and chaos will result. That is why everyone needs to be involved and each employee becomes the steward of their own responses, play times, and fun efforts.

- The trust-to-play model is about making a cultural commitment to the business. Like at Peppercomm, if you are not willing to take part in stand-up comedy, then you are not truly committed or like at Zappos when they offer you money to quit.
- Decide what the standard operating procedure is for play at work. Pick a theme that will resonate with your employees. Decide what sort of welcome wagon of fun you are going to present to a new employee to set the tone.
- Building a playful business culture is not a science. I cannot give you an exact formula for creating performance, but I can give you insight into your approach. A systematic approach based on transformative play will work.
- The final phase of building a performance culture is to give employees the freedom to begin living. Define what that means to your company, and ask for employee input to make your definitions clearer.

---

22 Richard Buckminster Fuller, http://www.goodreads.com/author/quotes/165737.Richard_Buckminster_Fuller
23 Charles Green, Trust and the Sharing Economy: A New Business Model, http://trustedadvisor.com/articles/trust-and-the-sharing-economy-a-new-business-model

Always remember to inspire those around you so that you can spread your message via institutionalization. I like to think of inspiration as the match and the people in your company as a candle. If they get it, then you will succeed. If they do not get it, no amount of strategy is going to help you transform that company.

For companies to make the leap from good to great, they have to consider these higher level methods of trust. If you do not trust your employees to follow the rules and still have enormous amounts of fun, you will send out the message that at any time someone could overstep their mark and get fired.

The Play–Purpose Connection

My wife makes the most amazing Thanksgiving ham. I asked her one day, "Cheris, why do you cut off the end of your famous Thanksgiving ham?" She looked at me and responded, "That's how my mom does it." So I decided to call her mother. "Mom, why do you cut off the end of your famous Thanksgiving ham?" She, too, replied, "That's how my mother does it." So I called Grandma. "Grandma, why do you cut off the end of your famous Thanksgiving ham?" Grandma instantly replied, "It's to make the ham fit in the only pan I have."

This is a great little example of how practices can be perpetuated by others without clear reasons on why they are done. My wife and her mother both cut the ends off for no reason. They were simply following instructions. In business, "pointless" instructions like these are everywhere—in business processes, in systems—all over the place.

Your organization needs to realize that it has to change before your people do. This is the play–purpose connection that has to happen. Your business wants the positive benefits from play, so they need to adjust their ways. This will mean revamping old "pointless" systems and replacing them with new, exciting methods of working.

If the symbols of your organization do not communicate and cultivate play, then you need to ask yourself (and your bosses) these questions:

- Do you know what you stand for?
- Do your structures and systems reflect a basic paradigm of purposeful play?
- Do you have a visually noticeable culture of play?
- Do you listen to each other's ideas?
- Can you make and admit mistakes?
- Can you engage with tough issues in a playful way?
- Do you have a culture of caring for the people in your company?
- Do you care about your work, your employees, and your reputation?
- Can you deliver value? Are you continuously improving and innovating?
- Can you reinvent yourself, and is your organization getting results?

All of these questions will help direct you on your path to redefining your company culture. If you lack in any of these areas, this is the best place to begin to create alignment and a sense of organizational play. Even if you are not the CEO, you can still influence others.

Set examples of play and caring—remember the impact one person can have on others and how it trickles down. (My wife's grandma proves it!) You can provide ongoing training and mentorship to keep people on the right paths. Once you are wearing your play glasses, you will see the impact of strengthening the value of productive play in your organization.

PLAY

Even Albert Einstein said that play is the highest form of research. For a man with such creative hair, he understood a thing or two about being productive. You need to give your employees courage and purpose so that they will play on their own. It will come with time as long as you continue to work on reshaping your business culture.

07

Influencing and Connecting With Play

"It's more fun when you're not the only one having it."

BERNIE DEKOVEN

When you have put in the time to reshape your business culture, the onus then falls on you to be the ambassador of play and to help others connect and share in meaningful ways. That means that you need to learn how to be an influencer and how to influence others to pass on the message of fun and productive play.

Play is always great when you are alone, but with others, it can be magic. In fact, the more people involved, the less time is required to have fun. This chapter is going to explore how you can be more of an inspiring playful leader and connect with others.

The Things About Humor You Never Knew

During one of my workshops I discovered that a participant—Clayton—was engaged. I congratulated him and then asked him how long he had been engaged. "Three years," he replied. I paused, repositioned my stance to look directly at him, and said, "Well, let's not rush into anything!" The class laughed.

I could have congratulated him and moved on, but I saw an opportunity for a playground moment. These little moments of fun add up, and they are your greatest asset. I want my classes to have fun and play. I believe that when they do, they learn more. It is time to stop taking yourself so seriously and to take fun seriously. Because fun is serious business.

- Did you know that humor goes a long way to making you a leader who is likable, understanding, and open and who has the ability to motivate people? A dynamic, playful spirit gets the best response from teams time and time again.
- Michael Kerr[24] says that the type or amount of humor in any given workplace depends entirely on their culture. Workplaces that encourage people to be themselves and that are less hierarchical and more innovative tend to produce more humor.
- Humor is also a powerful attraction tool. It involves others, reaches out to them, and invites them to be humorous too—and it can even unlock the play instinct in people that openly disagree with play at work.
- Humor influences behavior economics! Gentrification shifts the focus from just behavior to behavior and experience. It tries to affect an outcome, using a journey

---

[24] Jacquelyn Smith, 10 Reasons Why Humor Is a Key to Success at Work, http://www.forbes.com/sites/jacquelynsmith/2013/05/03/10-reasons-why-humor-is-a-key-to-success-at-work/

that evolves, engages the participant, and tries to create a sense of fun.
- Once again, humor has the very real power to keep people loyal to subject matter, a brand, or to a prescribed identity. Think employee retention and stronger leaders.

It is true that humor has the ability to help you influence and connect, but it is also an asset in your leaders and a great feature in your business culture, and it attracts people, influences their behavior, and keeps them on your side. Money can barely claim such amazing results!

Play as a Way To Bring People Together

Occasionally, I will poke fun at stragglers when they come late to a keynote event. I will make my way to the back of the room and banter about the "prime real estate"—often exclaiming how I bet they had to get there early for such choice spots. As I move around the room, I catch their attention, and make my way over to them. "Excuse me, sir!" I will say.

After the "Who me?" gesture, I ask them to stand. Then I ask them their name, how they are doing, and if they have any questions so far about my presentation. I once got a really clever response, "Yes, I do actually have a question. Can I please sit down?" The audience laughed. This type of play bonded me with the audience.

Play is a way of bringing people together. When there is no engagement with the crowd, they are just a crowd of spectators. When you engage with them and make them laugh, they become an audience.

Play has this great way of collapsing the power distance between people. When the audience member replied, he only did so because he was openly invited to exchange witty banter with me, even though I was on stage in a position of authority.

One of the best things about humor is its innate ability to reduce social distance. Connecting to people through serious fun will always involve humor. I am not talking about inappropriate or insensitive humor. Women use humor to build solidarity, while men use it to impress and emphasize similarities in each other.

But aggressive or modeless forms of humor must be prohibited. Either everyone enjoys the humor or it should not exist. That means if a joke is offensive or ugly, it is not funny, because there is someone who is harmed by it. All forms of that humor are not welcome in the workplace, because then it will force people to recede instead of connect.

- Humor is the most humanizing element of business that exists. It is a social catalyst, allowing everyone to find common ground in an instant.[25]
- Play is also a great ice breaker, and it helps put people at ease in social situations. No matter your job title, everyone is the same when you are playing. Laughter also facilitates divergent thinking, which is the ability to think about things from multiple perspectives.

Play is a team sport and works best in groups. When applying play dynamics to a business process or to your business as a whole, you need to understand the complexity of the rules that govern your organization. People remember how you made them feel.

If you can continually make your employees feel appreciated, amused, engaged, and light-hearted, they will enjoy it and pass it on to others. Play is viral like that! The happier you make your employees, the happier your customers become. It is a great system to test, and it feels brilliant when your results are confirmed.

---

[25] Dr Eric, Romero, Humor...The Social Catalyst at Work, http://competeoutsidethebox.com/wp-content/uploads/articles/Humor%20the%20Social%20Catalyst%20at%20Work.pdf

Breaking Down Boundaries: Play and Teamwork

For The Playful Leader, play also breaks down boundaries—which is an essential tool if you want to be effective at building quality, collaborative teams. For teamwork, there is no better learning tool than play. It teaches your teams how to engage with others, how to be friends, how to disagree, and how to work together as a solid unit.

Ever wonder why Disney is seen as the land of fun? Their whole strategy is to exceed their guests' expectations. And they do this through emotions, play, and humor. You do not even see the tactics that they employ, even though they are a very detail-oriented brand.

In their lost teddy bear story, the teddy bears all ended up on the bed watching the Disney Channel to the surprise of the family when they returned to their Disney property hotel room. They infuse everything with a sense of fun, magic, and possibility—and it has always been what makes this brand great.

- Energy is the capacity to do work. It is also your most precious resource, and it is totally squandered in the modern workplaces of today.
- Energy is actually four dimensional—physical, emotional, mental, and spiritual. Businesses have always sought to manage and monitor time but not energy. The irony, of course, is that energy needs to be managed to effectively use time!
- Play does not only produce energy in items that are being played with, it also produces positive energy in people.[26]

---

26 Susan Heathfield, 7 Ways to Foster Employee Motivation – Today, http://humanresources.about.com/od/motivationrewardretention/a/employee_motivation.htm

Play generates energy, and energy is the capacity to work. In other words, the more we play, the more we work.

When your teams play together, they learn to work together in the most incredible ways. Break down the barriers with a little levity before expecting employees to jump up and team up. They do not know each other as well as you think. Everyone needs a chance to get to know others. They need to understand who, why, and when if play and teamwork are involved.

The positive consequences of workplace fun can show up in customer satisfaction after the trickledown effect. Southwest Airlines actively practices and passionately encourages a culture of fun on the job, and they beat their competition every year in customer satisfaction surveys.

When your teams are energized and focused from the play they have just experienced, they will be more inclined to dedicate a good amount of work and effort to their customers. Brands that can share their playful culture get the best rewards—customers that come back over and over and develop real loyalty towards the brand.

The best advice that you can get is to start managing the energy levels of your teams by integrating play into their day. It will quickly translate into productivity, better customer service, and a happier, healthier workforce.

The Serious Act of Team-Based Fun

Fun increases with the willingness of staff to serve customers. Rogers Insurance, a company in Calgary, uses fun as one of their core values to motivate their 165 employees. Lindsey Mather, Vice President of Human Resources, said, "When you are having fun at work, you are in a better mood. You treat your clients better. The employees get along with each other better.

It is important in everything we do."[27]

Rogers Insurance developed a new position, "Director of Humor," that they have assigned to an existing employee—who is paid a generous lump sum above their regular salary—to plan fun and funny things for the workplace. The company also has a fun squad that is dedicated to making the lives of each employee a little happier.

Humor is a serious business because it invokes the chicken and egg ideology—forming a closed loop that keeps businesses successful. You see, when employees have fun, they work harder and smarter and make customers happy, which results in success. But the end result of a successful workplace is fun and happiness. The core issue has always been play and how it is instituted in teams.

Fun in the workplace is about building serious skills and developing habits that encourage you to enjoy your work. While ice cream Fridays are awesome, they may not be the best tactic for promoting team-based fun. A shared experience is always good, but a shared activity is better, especially if it invokes a desirable emotional state.

Taking time out to have fun has brought about better productivity. People should be free to customize their space, just like they would do at home. This is an individual freedom that promotes team connection because it invites everyone to share pieces of themselves with others in the business.

Gostick[28] and Christopher reveal that levity minded employees tend to climb the corporate ladder faster, they make more money than their co-workers, and they close more sales.

---

27 Mario Toneguzzi, Companies Using Humour to Grow Business, http://www.calgaryherald.com/business/Companies+using+humour+grow+business/9284763/story.html

28 The Fun Workplace May Be the Most Productive – New York Times, http://blog.miodragkostic.com/2008/04/

They also have real hair because a sense of humor reduces their stress levels.

The question remains—how do you bring play into your average work day? Consider that work and play are mutually supportive. Play breeds creativity, and it is the common link between both work and play. Forming new relationships between concepts, people, and things can inspire play because it is creative, which is closely linked to work.

Initially, introduce your teams to creative exercises, and slowly start adding in fun elements until your team is doing it on their own. From there, you can inspire the spread of fun, which as you know, is a very serious act indeed. This is even more true when you consider that other people will be involved.

Fair Play: Power Dynamics at Work

I have learned two things recently from the homeless. As I was crossing a street in downtown Salt Lake City, I noticed a homeless man ahead of me with a typical homemade cardboard sign. I wondered what it would say. I smiled as I approached and read, "Too ugly to prostitute, please help!" I gave him a dollar.

Crossing the street in downtown Denver, I noticed the second homeless man ahead. In my rush to get to a conference, I had left my coat at the hotel. As I approached the homeless man, he said, "Hey man, where is your coat? Don't you know it is cold out here?" I appreciated his concern and gave him a dollar.

On both occasions, I was superior to the homeless men. On both occasions, they managed to break through my innate "avoidance" of homeless types with wit and humor. It proves that even in the most desolate places, psychologically, humor always works. First you lift someone's spirits then they feel more inclined to help you, or work, or do something else.

Humor in the workplace can be more than awkward between

bosses and co-workers. Employees tend to laugh at anything a boss says, while they prevent themselves from truly engaging in fun because they are so on their guard.

- In the new generation, the influence of games on their expectations of work and life cannot be underestimated. If you leverage games to engage this generation, it will increase engagement of young employees.
- Employees of all ages find games engaging and fun. Play is a normal part of being a human being, and it will bring people together that have to work collaboratively on a specific task.

Play unifies an individual's various personas to guide growth, behavior, and engagement. They literally become more "themselves" when play is involved. Isolated play opportunities can be effective, but an integrated approach with performance incentives has the chance of yielding more than just incremental improvements.

Play disregards age and status and brings different minds together—which can result in extraordinary collaborations and opportunities for your company.

How to Influence With Fun

I was once invited to speak at a leadership training event at the Mandalay Bay Hotel in Las Vegas, the entertainment capital of the world. The day before the conference, participants and invited vendors were surprised by Jay Leno and a team of Clydesdale horses, who made their way into the conference room (yes, Jay was now out of work).

The next day, it was time for me to go on stage. The meeting planner wanted me to run on stage. The music started with "Let's Get It Started" by The Black Eyed Peas, and I started to run onto the stage and stopped halfway, bent over my knees, and pretended to pant.

The audience laughed. The music stopped, and everyone applauded even though I had not done anything yet. I played with the audience of 400 people, joking about Sin City by saying, "Ready to have fun? This is Las Vegas; you've been having fun since the moment you arrived! Raise your hand if you have already started to have fun." They laughed.

"Raise your hand if you've noticed the slot machines!" They laughed. "Raise your hand if you've lost any money yet." They laughed again. "Raise your hand if you are not done!" They laughed harder. "Sure, it's your recreation or entertainment budget, though, right?" Then I started my speech. Play connects with people and audiences of all sizes.

- Occasionally play games that involve every single person in the entire company, with one clear winner. It promotes organizational cohesiveness.
- Do a leaders roast, where the people in your company create harsh jokes about the bosses and then stage a panel show while everyone watches and laughs.
- Have fun theme days with costumes, and name different rooms unique and funny titles. If you can, dedicate a room to gaming, playing, and goofing off.

If fear is a very big problem (because your company has some very stern leadership structures), start by breaking down the perceptions about fear. Humanize your leadership, give them flaws and opinions outside of work, and show your employees that they can be themselves without fear.

Exploring the Relationship Between People and Play

The number one factor that motivates employees to create great experiences for your customers is "having fun at work." Not career advancement or job security or recognition—simply having fun. This applies to the employee customer experience as customers can instantly tell how your employee representative feels about them.

When you make it all right to play at work, it becomes all right to play with customers—which leads to stronger, better, and longer-lasting consumer relationships and overall experiences.

Viable Alternatives

Scientifically speaking, these are the reasons why so many CEOs and brands are sitting up and taking notice of fun and humor as a viable alternative to old business models and methods.

- Casual banter builds relationships and helps people work together more creatively. You transform your employees into players when you make communication all right in the workplace—even the silly kind.
- Involving the customer in your fun makes them more than just your customer; it makes them a part of your business culture—which directly translates into higher revenues over time.
- Humor has the power to keep people loyal, to help people bond, and to collapse power distances that we have spoken about before.

In a world where stress, overworking, and crushing, debilitating workloads are common, it seems as though humor is the antidote to many of these recurring problems. The Playful Leader will reduce sick day rates on enjoyment alone.

Evidence That Fun Promotes Personal Growth

Personal growth is something that leaders are always pursuing in one way or another. The more you grow, the better your chances of getting promoted or excelling in the company that you are in. Fun happens to be one of the motivators for personal growth, which means that more leaders will spring up from your employee ranks.

It also means that you will be fully energized and primed to grow whenever you need to. Success depends on you effectively assessing the very best that each employee has to offer and then enabling them to have the highest possible levels of engagement.

In other words, when you have fun, you greatly accelerate the rate at which you are able to grow on a personal level. This is great news for you as a playful leader, but it is also great news for your employees and customers. These individuals will also absorb more when they encounter your play processes or fun culture.

- Employees will be motivated to grow and reach for more, and they will learn faster, which is of huge benefit to your company.
- Customers will retain more critical information about your brand and products when they engage with your employees in a fun way. Ever hear that old adage "top of mind, top of sales"? It applies.

Just imagine what fun and play can do for your senior leadership! It will open their eyes to new opportunities in your niche, make them more susceptible to modern suggestions, and may even convince them to make the total shift to a playful business culture.

The Best Ideas in Life Come From Play

I have never met a customer that did not enjoy a good chuckle.

Even the stern types appreciate the right kind of humor. It transcends race, age, nationality, and class distinctions.

It was John Cleese who once said, "If I can make you laugh with me, you like me better, which makes you more open to my ideas. If I can get you to laugh at a particular point that I make, by laughing at it, you acknowledge that it's truth."

And that is what play is all about. It opens doors on every level, psychologically, emotionally, spiritually, and physically. It is the only thing that spreads like wildfire and can instantly align an entire group of people with what you are trying to communicate.

The best ideas in life come from play. There are so many examples of this throughout history that it is quite insane that we have never had play as a part of our work days before. Speaking broadly, there are three states that we all exist in: doing, thinking, and being.[29]

- Doing requires you to already be engaged in something that is taking up your time, energy, and resources. It is not ideal for idea generation.
- Thinking requires you to think about things from different perspectives, but our thoughts are naturally narrow and unreliable, and we can get stuck on ideas.
- There is another state that we enter when we are not thinking and not doing; "autopilot" is another word for it. When you have been driving for a long time and suddenly you "wake up" and realize that you were driving, this is when you have become so bored you have slipped into that "being" state.

---

29 Steve Taylor, The Secret of Success: Relax and Do Nothing, http://www.psychologytoday.com/blog/out-the-darkness/201401/the-secret-success-relax-and-do-nothing

The great thing about being is that it brings us into the present. When your brain is relaxing and doing something that is not that important (like play or fun), you slip into these states more often. The irony is that your subconscious mind continues to search for solutions when you are not actively dwelling on them.

That is why you might be watering the plants one day and that marketing solution comes to you out of the blue. The Western culture idealizes the first two states and basically ignores the third, even though evidence suggests real genius and brilliance comes from that state.

On a spiritual and psychological level, "being" has fuelled some of the greatest discoveries in history. Newton discovered gravity in this state while lazing under a tree. Rene Descartes was half asleep in bed when coordinate geometry came to him. The biggest and best ideas sneak up on you when you play, have fun, and relax.

The fact that we have not played means that for the past several decades, our working lives have been consumed by thinking and doing, which has effectively crowded out our natural genius—or the natural genius in everyone.

If you can create playground moments that give your customers the chance to participate, make choices, and interact with employees, they will ultimately connect with the experience and form a bond with the company providing that experience. Likability matters!

- Provide your employees and customers with confidence, intrigue, interest in others, enthusiasm, and respect, and they will like you.

Types of Play and Humor to Avoid

With that in mind, there are some real potholes on the road to becoming a playful leader. There are some types of play and humor that you need to avoid. Imagine that these forms of humor are the ghosts and your employees are Pac-Man. They will gobble up all of the delicious nuggets of fun and humor until something causes a hostile experience.

- Aggressive humor[30] is the type that you really want to watch out for. This form of "play" is used to criticize, manipulate, and degrade others by teasing, sarcasm, and open ridicule. Also called "put down" humor, there is often a target—and that target has to endure some fairly embarrassing or hurtful comments.

Your company should have a zero tolerance policy on overtly aggressive humor and play. Anything involving physical, emotional, or psychological distress; bullying; teasing; or straight out name-calling must be removed from your play ideals.

- It is never okay to force anyone to engage in play if they do not want to. Ever. Peer pressuring someone to do it can end up in people resigning because their wishes are not respected. Play is meant to be fun, not hostile.
- Play may not be overtly physical or cause anyone harm or duress. At any time, an individual can point out that someone has crossed the line, and in that event, steps should be taken to sort out the problem verbally.
- Humor often borders on sarcasm, irony, and some not-so-acceptable work topics. While some mild versions of this are all right, it should be made clear that you are not comedians and that "shock" humor is not welcome at work.
- Taste is something to be considered in your company.

---

30 Louise Dobson, What's Your Humor Style, http://www.psychologytoday.com/articles/200606/whats-your-humor-style

Different brands will have different comedic preferences. A prank at a tech startup may be great, but pull the same prank on a financial advisor at a law firm and consequences could result.

Find out what your brand's style of humor is and how it can best be expressed using play and the interactions of the employees in your company. Soon you will realize that you all enjoy a particular type of humor and that it works well.

08

Playing Hard With Organizational Change

"When we engage in what we are naturally suited to do, our work takes on the quality of play and it is play that stimulates creativity. So play with your intuition."

LINDA NAIMAN

I like to believe that the kid that played hardest in kindergarten was the guy who eventually grew up to own the most successful businesses. My belief is not based on assumption but rather an interesting theory relating to play.

Just like that kid who was always having the most fun at playtime, they managed to retain this childlike experience into adulthood and eventually translate it into money. A lot of money. Because the bottom line is that playful companies function better on every level.

How Cognitive Fitness and Play Go Hand in Hand

Remember the Blue Man Group? They started a school! There, they teach their students to play and create simultaneously. It is quite inspiring to think about when you consider that this is an extreme form of creative play set in front of thousands of people.

With things like unchartered play, imaginative play, and unleashing the power of play being a core concern in business these days, it is great to know that there are real cognitive benefits[31] involved in play.

Corporations face a blinding and fast-moving rate of change that they need to be prepared for. Companies recognize that if they want to "survive and thrive" in a global marketplace, they have no choice but to be able to adapt quickly. Employees resist change, which is always a secondary concern.

The most important thing to note is that human capital is finally getting the attention that it deserves. Ways and new systems built to connect and engage with people will save companies billions. All we have right now is the cognitive fitness that play induces.

An individual's brain needs to be flexible, quick, and sharp in order to comprehend and engage in play with others. In negative situations, The Playful Leader will be more adept at using fun and humor to help others recognize a more positive reality.

Old wisdom tells us that there are two kinds of people: those that look for miracles and find them and those that do not look for miracles and never see them. The same is true for humor in life. If you look for it and expect it, you will find it. But if you are closed off from it, it does not matter if there is a Disney parade in your front garden; you will not see it.

---

[31] Roderick Gilkey, Cognitive Fitness, http://hbr.org/2007/11/cognitive-fitness/ar/1

It is true that play improves and expands your mind, your thinking capability, and even the way you relate to other people. So change the game—disrupt it! You have to innovate and change the game according to this new set of rules.

The Mechanics of Play in a Business Environment

Five minutes before I was due to kick off a training session with executives from New York, my laptop computer died. I began to panic, sweat, and generally have a nervous breakdown. Then I announced, "Our topic is change, and we will begin in five minutes, but can somebody please help me change by letting me use your laptop? You see, mine just died."

Laughter filled the room, and I realized that it was going to be okay. Somebody once said laughter is the best medicine. It made me feel a lot better. In any business environment, you will need to establish the mechanics of play—or the "playbook," as I call it. These are the rules that you will build into your organizational structure to embrace change.

- Busting silos and opening up the organization will help you get the best ideas from everywhere—your management, your employees, and your consumers.
- Remove the mental crud from your mind, and realize that you need play and creativity to transcend your limitations in this new, competitive market.
- Believe in the power of the unexpected, and unlock creative energy. Imagination and creativity are central to innovation. Playing actively engages the creative side of your brain. When you are fully engaged in play, you drop some of those psychological barriers and stop censoring and editing your thoughts.

- People think more clearly and operate more productively when they have had a break to clear the cobwebs in their brains. Take short breaks, and encourage your teams to start doing the same thing!

Google gets over a million job applications every year. Only 0.5%, or 5000, of those applicants ever make it. What makes Google such a desirable company to work for? Google understood from the beginning that fun and progress are what produce productivity and profit. To be this way does not cost the business money at all.

It is about investing in nonmonetary things like employee creativity, engagement, and the need to matter among their peers. By playing more, you engage the creative side of your brain on whatever task you focus on—which creates new possibilities, solutions, and ideas.

A Cornell University study[32] found that people who had just seen a funny movie increased their creative flexibility.

The Positive Reality: Turning Negatives Into Positives

Fun and play at work actually give you, The Playful Leader, some secret powers. Like a super hero, it allows you to swoop in and turn negatives into positives in nearly any situation—whether it is between employees, between a customer and an employee, or between a manager and an employee.

Humor should be considered as an energizing force in the workplace that stimulates creativity, ultimately leading to a vibrant work environment, greater service delivery, and a more productive organization. You might have a pleasant workplace

---

[32] Anthony Gemma, Making People Smile Program, http://www.anthonygemma.com/PDF_FunProgramLaunch.pdf

environment right now, but it is not anywhere near as positive as it could be.

- Imagination and exploration need to be encouraged so that when problems arise, they are dealt with swiftly and fairly.
- Amazing ideas have something in common with bad ideas—they both sound ridiculous early on, so keep that in mind for your employees.
- Everyone wants to improve, but few want to change. A curious, creative, and fun working environment gives people the ability to improve along positive lines without having to suppress their natural inclinations to pursue who they are.
- Change your organizational question from "How long will this take?" to "How far can I go?" to place the emphasis back on your human capital.
- Innovation is a practice, not an idea. In negative environments, you cannot see innovation. Promote the right employee mindsets to get the modern results that you need from your innovative employees.

Business thinking is about removing ambiguity and driving results. You need to get rid of those old practices that are doing more harm than you think. These "negatives" are increasing your staff turnover, losing you valuable employee talent, and slowing down your employees' ability to get things done.

Business thinking and routine work may be a rigid process, but innovation is not. It requires a willingness to bend the rules for the right reasons. You need to branch out, have fun, and get your staff involved in this positive mindset.[33] Innovations

---

33   Jon Gordon, Positive Thinking Is Contagious, http://www.guideposts.org/positive-thinking/power-positive-thinking-work

almost never happen alone; they come by shared insight and the non-judgmental sharing of ideas.

You and your team should aspire to be strategic thinkers. Albert Einstein once said, "Any man who reads too much and uses his brain too little falls into lazy habits of thinking." You cannot simply study play and having fun; you have to think these models and structures through yourself and come up with innovative ways to employ them in your company.

Get your team members involved. When your teams are involved, they add so many positive dynamics to the play process.

The Miracle of Fun Story

While visiting the Thomas Edison National Historic Park home residence in Glenmont, New Jersey, I thought it was interesting that directly next to the library was a room named "the thought parlor." I like to imagine the time Edison spent there putting ideas and information together. This is where possibilities were born in Edison's mind.

When John Donahoe, CEO of eBay, was asked who his biggest competitor was, he said innovation. If a competitor of his becomes more innovative than the team at eBay, they may lose their business, or at least a large portion of it. Innovation is relentless, and it never stops moving forward. With each passing day, it becomes a larger concern for companies.

The real miracle of fun is that it gives birth to new innovation wherever it goes. And innovation is an act of leadership. The more leaders that create a culture of innovation, the more people are energized and innovating—creating a living ecosystem that builds on itself. At the same time, it forces progress to spin at a blistering rate.

That is why so many companies are embracing play—because if they do not embrace it now, they may fall prey to progress and be innovated out of the market. For many brands, it is their absolute worst fear. A lack of innovation impedes an organization from thriving, so not only do you fall behind, you become obsolete.

Fun can change all that for your company. With play and regular fun, you can collectively harness the power of every employee until you have access to a cooperation of minds that are all working towards the betterment of your business. That is right! You have to play your way to innovation[34] and growth in your organizational structure.

This might mean instituting programs that focus on mental training, rehearsal, and assessments that are ongoing so that you can get the most out of your employees. When you are never having fun or playing at work, your thoughts become parked in the disabled zone. You need a psychological crowbar to pry open that vehicle and drive your mind to warmer climates, where it is free to be creative.

To change your thinking, change the kind of questions that you ask. Dig deeper, and really try to unveil what makes you and your teams special and innovative. For The Playful Leader, the real miracle of fun is in sharing it with others.

You will see how much of a difference it makes in your own life, and then you will be able to share it with everyone you care about at work. Not only that, but it will help you repair the damage that a boring, stuffed shirt workplace has done to its employees, transforming them back into human capital, a ready-made think tank, and innovators of the best kind.

The Game: How to Put Fun in It

Have you ever tried to change the way you think about thinking? It is darn near impossible if innovation, creativity, and the right

---

34   Corporate Innovation, http://www.nifplay.org/opportunities/corporate-innovation/

mindset are absent. Work is like a hamster wheel. Every day you get on the wheel, and it spins according to the way that it was bolted in place inside the cage. This imagery became so real people have been calling it the "rat race."

Day after day, it is always the same. This is the game that is work. Unfortunately, the game has lacked rules, locations, players, and many other elements that could have made it exciting. Now imagine if every day that hamster got into the wheel and took off to another location to meet other hamsters on other wheels to make extraordinary things happen.

This is what fun does for your employees. It releases them from the hamster wheel of work. It lets them pick their paths, find new directions, and enjoy the work that they do for you. This helps them see things that others do not so that they can innovate for you in original ways.

Every employee on that hamster wheel only needs some play to make it worthwhile. Hook up those wheels to some generators, and create some new ideas! Responding to change is one critical skill that organizations cannot be without. But actually creating and implementing real change—well, you need the tool to loosen the bolts.

Innovation,[35] creativity, and collaboration are those tools—all brought about because you allowed the hamsters to roam free and have some good times. If you can incorporate play into your innovation process, you are going to make it more enjoyable and you will get better results. Plus, innovation breeds innovation, so you will want to gain momentum there.

Putting "fun" in the game of work is hard work. I imagine it is like walking into your living room only to find that someone has changed the wallpaper and rearranged the furniture. Figuring

---

35 Michael Graber, Jocelyn Atkinson, The Role of Play in Innovation, http://www.memphisdailynews.com/news/2014/jan/27/the-role-of-play-in-innovation/

out whether it looks better or worse is not the first reaction. The very first reaction is "How dare they! Someone changed everything!"

You have to grow into the kind of leader who can ignite workplace enthusiasm, end the culture of endless rules and routine, and delight people with a fresh look at play, innovation, and creativity. The wheel always spins faster when there is somewhere to go.

Play as a tool for innovation is truly what the game is about. Getting the most creative value out of your team, for your organization is where your company's future lies. Never underestimate the emergence of the creative economy. People will determine which businesses thrive and which fail in the future.

The only question that remains is if your company will realize the potential of play so that you can begin harnessing the power of innovation long before you are overwhelmed by the competition. Living is about work–play balance. It is all a part of one life.

Forcing Fun: The Dos and Don'ts

There is an old fable about the space race of the 1960s. NASA was faced with a pretty huge problem. Astronauts needed a pen that would write in the endless vacuum of space. NASA worked for months on the project, spending millions on developing this pen. It had special pressurized ink cartridges and would write perfectly in space...the Russians used a pencil.

The lesson, of course, is that sometimes businesses spend an enormous amount of time, energy, and resources on the wrong idea without even realizing that a simple solution would work if they only thought outside the box. If you want to teach your employees these lessons, you need to know the dos and don'ts of forcing fun.

PLAY

You cannot—by definition—force fun on people, because fun is a natural process that happens when play, enjoyment, and relaxation are all happening concurrently. Try to force it, and it just becomes another form of work and punishment.

- Do always allow your employees to choose their level of fun, when they want to engage, and where. Encourage them and work with them—but never force them.
- Do not embarrass shy employees by making them play games, engage in fun, or take part in competitions where they stand no chance of winning.
- Do support any ideas that your employees have for fun. Help your employees institute their ideas so that everyone can enjoy a closer, happier workplace.
- Do not allow certain employees with more "outgoing" natures to seize control of play and dominate. Many will try, but you have to make it clear that play is for everyone.
- Do allow every individual the chance to have an opinion about play despite what anyone else on the team may say. Validation is important, and even if they point blank refuse to play, their feelings are relevant.
- Do not make employees feel left out by forming cliques of players in the workplace. Everyone needs to be involved, whether they watch, participate, help create, cheer, or record the results of play.

09

Leveling the Playing Field: Take Action!

"Work made fun gets done."

DAVID FAIRHURST

When you invest in play and strategic fun, it pays off big time. It pays to play. The technical difficulties come in when you want to level the playing field and act on your theories, models, structures, and research.

Play is a great concept, but it is so much more when you actually get it going. It gains momentum and touches every facet of your company life. I strongly encourage you to pursue the implementation of play structures with serious dedication.

Putting Play Principles Into Action

One day after giving my early teenage son, Carson, a list of jobs to do that day, he told me how he felt. He said, "Dad, I hate work! And I will always hate work!" I looked at him and replied, "Someday you will thank me." He muttered something unintelligible and stormed off as teenage boys do when they do not understand things.

About six months later Carson and I were building a large storage shed for my father. We were doing the roof, and if you have ever done that, you know that putting shingles on a roof on a hot day is one of the least glamorous or enjoyable jobs ever created by man.

We were about halfway done when Carson suddenly looked back and said, "Dad, this is fun." "What did you say?" I asked him. "This is fun," he repeated. I could see from his facial expression that he was proud of what we had accomplished so far. When I reminded him that this was work and he said it was fun, he was not ready to thank me yet. But the point is that any task can be reframed and enjoyed with a bit of play. That is why you need to put play principles into action when you step into the role of a playful leader.

- Play principles include having fun with peers, customers, and managers. You will need to devise methods of playing with these people in a constructive way.
- Put the ball in other people's court. Be playful, and wait for their playful response. See if you can generate any momentum with what you are trying to achieve.
- Focus on unexpected, surprise-based fun. This can be the most pleasing as it is not expected and therefore there is no pressure when it happens. Be spontaneous for your employees by letting them experience new things.

Imagine that play is like an ocean. You may drift from here to there, but you should make sure that you are always on course according to what has happened to you. Create a playbook for your organization, and fill it with all the great ideas that your employees have.

Host productive play training workshops to educate your staff. Smile, raise your eyebrows, and be vocal—these are all elements of sustainable play. The systems and infrastructure that you will eventually build will all be shaped around the experiences that you have and the contributions that you collect from your employees. Let them help you!

How to Build Players for Game Time

There is nothing more fun than the celebration of success. Celebrations in general should be embraced by your company. Birthdays, anniversaries—these are dates that matter in the lives of your employees. You need to build each of these people into players so that they can enjoy game time when it happens.

- Get your players involved in the creation of your playbook. They will feel more engaged and part of the playful culture transition.
- Play often and at regular intervals. Do not set hard and fast rules about when; just place limitations on how long. Employees can choose to take their play however and whenever they see fit or when they need it most.
- Hire competent employees who already enjoy fun and have a good sense of humor. Appoint the people in your company with strong humor skills as members of your very own fun squad. Get them to engage other employees with fun.
- Top level management needs to show solidarity with you and this transition to a more playful culture. After the tests have proven that it works, come up with a way to humanize your leadership and get them involved in the game time process.

- Lift restrictions on emailing and social networking. Research by Christopher Robert[36] of Trulaske College of Business at the University of Missouri found that the type of humor that has the biggest impact on employee engagement was email humor.
- Pay attention during "play" times to see how your employees react. Make sure that anyone can come to you and complain and that they will not be seen as a Debbie Downer at all. It will be in the strictest confidence.
- Create opportunities for play by inviting employees' families and friends around to socialize and see the business culture.
- A specially prepared meeting that deals with the institution of playful culture is generally all that is needed to dispel any rumors or doubts about the process.

Finally, establish a fun committee or squad that organizes fun activities or experiences for your employees—in and out of the workplace. They need to be appropriate and enriching, and this committee will be headed up by someone that rotates ideas and keeps things fresh, new, and exciting.

You should also encourage spontaneity on the job because it is central to fun and play.

The Customer Wants to Play Too

Having barely passed the requirements to graduate from high school (perhaps the vice principal never wanted to see me again, so he pushed me through), graduation day finally arrived. Two of my friends and I decided that we would sing with the high school choir.

---

36 Bryan C Daniels, Light Humor in the Workplace Is a Good Thing, Says MU Business Professor, http://munews.missouri.edu/news-releases/2007/1030-robert-humor.php

One problem—we were not in the choir. We had not tried out, or been selected, or practiced a single song that the choir was going to sing. But it did not matter. Neil, Craig, and I were strategically seated (one on the left side, one in the middle, one on the right).

It came time for Mr. Tucker to bring the choir to their feet. He raised his hands as the choir stood up. I stood up. So did Neil. So did Craig. Then two of us got cold feet and sat back down. Not Craig. He was ready to stand and deliver.

Up he went, blending in nicely with the choir. He moved his lips and pretended to sing. To this day I doubt that Mr. Tucker picked up on this little stunt. Craig was ready to stand and deliver when an opportunity presented itself.

You will find that this happens a lot at work. Even the quietest people can sometimes feel inspired to act out of character if the right situation presents itself. But nowhere is this more prevalent than in your customer base.

When brands reach out with playfulness to customers, they often respond with excellent results. The stage just has to be set for them. Your company can do this by reaching out and engaging with playful media, initiatives, and events.

- Use eye contact and facial expressions to show interest in your customers and watch them to see how comfortable they are with engaging in a humorous way with your brand.
- Create attraction with friendly contact using excellent playful digital marketing strategies and real world events based around interactive play.
- Watch for cues of inclusion and exclusion. People that are included maintain eye contact, while those that are not look away or down. People need to feel acknowledged if they are to participate in something fun.

Include your customers in your playful new culture by getting them involved. Let them play with you.

Playing games[37] with your customers inspires brand connections and long-term relationships, and you know what? It helps customers like you more. That way they will buy more from you over time and support your community with renewed gusto.

Five Play Strategies to Use

There are five great play strategies that you can use to engage with your employees and customers. These have been tested, and they work. Keep in mind that scheduling the fun can reduce stress levels. Some employees find surprise experiences rather stressful!

1. To make things more exciting in the office, introduce friendly competitions with fun or unusual rewards. Start contests everyone can get in on, not just your sales teams. Contests can be specific—like best sales letter—or they can be broad—attitude of the week for example. Choose and rotate impartial judges, one per department.

2. Make fun a priority, but be careful of rigid structures. Google has multiple areas where different kinds of employees can cater to their own interests and needs based on what they prefer. You do not need to have a foosball table or a dartboard to have a fun workplace; you only need to look at what your employees need then build structures around that.

3. Integrate creative play into the work environment. Sometimes all it takes is one employee to champion

---

[37] Mitchell Osak, Gamification Unboxed: Should You Play Games With Your Customers, http://www.callcenter-iq.com/customer-experience/articles/gamification-unboxed-should-you-play-games-with-yo/

an initiative to get it done while on the job. If you are concerned about your employee becoming distracted by the play, think of the Colorado energy company that reduced unwanted turnover from 25% to 5% because of a new play model.

4. Move your meetings to be in different rooms or outside—or host them in weird and wonderful places. Museums, aquariums, and cafes are all great locations for meetings. You will enjoy meaningful conversations because the location is different, which inspires people. To sustain a sense of fun and performance, make your team care about your project.

5. Sustainable play in the workplace requires managing three key areas: tasks, environment, and relationships. Everyone should be responsible to do or to engage in one fun thing every day. Solo play can include setting individual challenges based on time or quality.

Food and drink plays a huge role in a company's efforts to have fun. Many employees would be happy with a muffin as the "fun" element in their day. It is sad that they are so deprived of fun that a baked item would make them so happy. But that is the world we live in! Devise strategies around food to enhance the fun that your employees have at work.

Short time outs stimulate productivity as well. Even a ten-minute break every two hours is enough to significantly boost the productivity of an individual. Speed, quality, and satisfaction all improve when these small breaks become mandatory.

Unexpected Surprises and Life Lessons

As a playful leader, you can bet that you will have a lot of unexpected surprises and life lessons to learn in your career. Some might take the form of your entire office being covered in tin foil, while others may be more serious (like a crying employee).

Here is how you should conduct yourself to face these challenges head on. They are coming, and they will be varied. Working with people is a lucky packet; you never know what you are going to get until you have received it.

- Always smile.
- Make everything a game if you can, and challenge yourself to come up with more creative ways of exploring different subjects, duties, and work flows.
- Be aware and be spontaneous, but notice when the people around you are not being quite as enthusiastic about what you are doing as you are.
- Make your own fun, own your fun, and share the fun that you own with others.
- Explore the pain of real life because there is humor in it. Convert this pain into humor, and use it as a pain killer to facilitate engagement with employees.
- Ideas are a dime a dozen, but it costs effort to implement an idea well. Focus on the execution, and do not compromise on your plans.
- Focus on managing your own energy and the energy expenditure of your employees.

The goal is always to create real fun, otherwise play does not work and there are no real benefits. This is perhaps the most dangerous pitfall of all, and it can come as a real surprise. The last thing you want is to institute play structures, and a few months later (when you think all is going swimmingly), a shark shows up in your office and devours your self-esteem.

You do not want to find out that people are not enjoying your play. Then you have not been paying enough attention to what they are saying and feeling and how they are reacting to your leadership. Curiosity will lead you down a lot of different humor paths, but as a rule, you need to authenticate these paths.

- Is this play structure really amusing/working/effective?
- Are people genuinely getting into it?

As you gain experience with play and using humor and fun to enhance your business culture, these elements will become your prominent concerns. Do not let them sneak up on you in surprise for a not-so-amusing life lesson!

10

Too Serious to Be Happy (Taking It Home)

> "Two roads diverged in a wood, and I—I took the one less traveled by, And that has made all the difference."
>
> ROBERT FROST

Are you a fan of fun? I mean real fun. The kind that you have when you are on holiday or with friends. If you are too serious, you cannot be happy. And while it is important to be serious about some things, it is far more important to be happy about everything.

If you can successfully spread play around the workplace, you will invite happiness back into your life and into the lives of your employees. Being happy is a business advantage and a direct result of play in the workplace.

How to Take Fun Home With You

While travelling to Phoenix, I had to use the restroom. As I walked into the restroom, I heard someone whistling. As I got closer, I could see that it was a custodian. He was whistling! What is whistling a sign of? That is right! It is a sign of happiness. The custodian was in a state of play.

He was totally happy to be cleaning those toilets. Now, if he can be happy cleaning toilets, then I can be happy doing some other (less horrific) mundane task...no matter what it is. I hope we can choose happiness, I hope that in our tasks we find purpose and meaning—and that happiness is what results.

I take fun very seriously, but I always joke about it because people recharge when they play. They gain energy when they are playing. Then they become happy and can spend that energy on work. But happiness stays long after the play is over. Employees take it home with them.

- When you are happy at work, you are happier at home—happier with your life, your kids, your family, and your hobbies. Play fuels happiness, and it leaks into every nook and cranny of your life.

- Laughter releases endorphins into your brain, which is why joking around with friends seems like so much fun. Fun is a critical component in the equation of living a happy life. To be fulfilled, you have to do a lot of small things during your day that increase your brain chemicals[38] and put you in a good mood. Fun actually fuels happiness, and you can take it home with you.

- When you enjoy your work and look forward to your day, something incredible happens. Your world opens up. You become primed to see the positive in life and to look for opportunities and positive experiences. That is why fun at work is so essential; it contributes towards the way you feel about your whole life.

---

38   Carolyn Gregoire, How to Wire Your Brain for Happiness, http://www.huffingtonpost.com/2013/10/17/how-tiny-joyful-moments-c_n_4108363.html

Taking fun home with you is a simple act of enjoying your day at work. With the right play programs in place, little amusements and delights during the day will culminate in a good mood, which will become happiness when you arrive at home. You will play and have more fun with your friends and family because play inspires more play.

The Seven Principles of Positive Psychology

As The Playful Leader, you already know that being positive fuels success and performance at work. It is the reason why you are so interested in learning how to play more often. There are seven principles of positive psychology[39] that contribute to this.

#1: Happiness is an advantage in life

Positive brains have a biological advantage over brains that are neutral or negative, which means that if you can train your brain to be more positive more often, you can actually train yourself to be happier and more productive and improve your performance levels.

#2: Your mindset controls your life

The second principle refers to how you innately experience the world around you. Your ability to succeed within it constantly changes based on your mindset. This principle proves that if you can adjust your mindset, you can reclaim the power to succeed at anything.

#3: The opportunity effect

When your brain gets stuck on certain patterns and trends that focus all of your energy on negativity, stress, and failure, you actually manifest these thoughts. This principle tells you

---

39 Happiness Advantage: The Seven Principles of Positive Psychology That Fuel Success and Performance at Work, http://learnbyblogging.com/?p=2535

that you can retrain your brain to spot these patterns and adjust them so that you can start to see opportunities instead of failures in the workplace.

#4: The falling up effect

When you experience failure, crisis, stress, and defeat, your brain maps different paths to help you cope. But this principle tells you that you need to find the mental path that leads you up and out of that state of suffering and teaches you to be happier.

#5: The perspective advantage

When you are faced with overwhelming challenges, your rational brain can often get eclipsed by your emotions. When this happens, you lose all perspective. This principle shows you how to regain that control by focusing on small goals that are achievable. Then you can widen the circle and see the big picture again.

#6: The twenty second rule

When a challenge lasts for a long time, it can feel impossible to complete. Human willpower is limited and directly related to the amount of energy that we have. When willpower fails, we fall back on old habits and take the path of least resistance. To avoid this, you need to take that twenty second window and replace bad habits with good ones.

#7: Invest in social support

When stress and challenges arise, most people recede and retreat into themselves. But the most successful people invest in their friends, peers, and family to get ahead. You need a social support network to stay positive and be happy.

These seven principles are great to know and will help you keep your mind straight when you are teaching others how to play, have fun, and stay positive at work.

Happiness in the Workplace

Even though the recession is several years past, there is statistical evidence that shows people in American companies are not happy. This has been attributed to the fact that a dwindling economy has forced people to stay in their current positions.

Without advancement, people have become trapped in their jobs. They say money cannot buy happiness, and that is true. But friends can buy happiness, according to a recent survey.[40]

The majority of people would turn down more money if it meant that they could continue working with friends. Clearly, social dynamics play a much larger part in the workplace than previously suspected.

The good news is that play facilitates a greater number of connections, which moves away from the previously siloed business models of yesterday. With these modes of play, employees will be able to meet people outside of their immediate location or department so that they can make more friends.

- Happy employees do not stay in one role for too long; they actively seek progress. There has to be potential for advancement for employees to remain happy. Staying in the same job for too long leads to burnout.
- There is no such thing as work–life balance, because work is part of your life and that life is supposed to be happy. That is why you need to play more at work—so that happiness can exist in the office and outside of the office. That is real happiness—when you can express yourself wherever you are.
- When employees are given the chance to do something

---

[40] Caroline Fairchild, Workplace Happiness Survey Finds Friends Are More Important Than Salary, http://www.huffingtonpost.com/2012/10/17/workplace-happiness-friends-over-salary_n_1971110.html

that has meaning, they become happier. This is because people seek meaning in the world, and many are attracted to opportunities that change the world for the better or the chance to make others happier. This is great for playful cultures.

- A playful workplace encourages collaboration, appreciation, and acknowledgement, which is a vital element in maintaining a happy work life. Employees are people, and they need to feel happy to produce the best work possible.

Happiness in the workplace is a serious advantage because it drives forward progress. A happy company keeps people working at their best and looking for solutions to make people even more comfortable or satisfied with their work. This is a great method of retaining employees and ensuring that trained talent stays in your company.

Happy employees are more mindful of the work they do and how they do it. They care more about the people around them and about their customers. This is all good news for a business that is about to institute play into your business model.

The Happier, More Productive Employee

Because you are going to be the model for all of your employees to emulate, it makes sense to focus on being a happier, more productive individual yourself. Your well-being depends on your ability to institute these programs effectively and remain in a playful mood.

By maintaining your own mood, you will teach others how to do the same. Here is how you can keep happy at work while still being productive and leading.

- *Do not perform the same routines every day.* Structures are great, but routine leads to monotony, which will drive you insane. Mix it up, take walks, vary your work routine to include new locations and types of work, and hang out in new places each day.

- *Get outside.* A brief walk outside with nature can do you a world of good. All you have to do is leave your office (yes, leave) and grab a friend or two. Go for a walk around the block or through the park to reenergize yourself.
- *Customize your work space.* Spend some time making your desk at work feel like home away from home—which it is because you spend most of your time at work. Family photos, posters, and objects that make you happy should be all around you to show off your personality to other people.
- *Meet new people.* Make a point every week of meeting new people. Challenge them to a game, or take part in an activity together. This will expose you to new opinions and will keep your creative energy high.
- *Do not forget to exercise.* Periodically stopping to exercise is a secret that executives hide away from other people. When they feel spent, they simply jump on the treadmill or get on an exercise bike to recharge. It improves their moods and facilitates health and wellness.

The more you focus on helping others achieve success with play, the better at it you will become. In this case, you will learn by teaching and experiencing these wonders for yourself. There are few things as amazing as seeing a whole company of people enjoy themselves, pull together, and unite as a happy brand.

The happier the people in the brand, the happier your customers will be. Happiness really does start from within—and once that is sorted out, only then can it filter over into your customers and partners. When they see how happy your employees are, they will want to be involved with what you have to offer.

> *"More than a decade of ground breaking research in the field of positive psychology and neuroscience has proven in no uncertain terms that the relationship between success and happiness works the other way around. Thanks to this cutting-edge science, we now know that happiness is the precursor to success, not merely the result. And that happiness and optimism actually fuel performance and achievement, giving us the competitive edge that I call the Happiness Advantage."*
> **SHAWN ANCHOR**

11

Becoming The Playful Leader in a Serious World

"We are never more fully alive, more completely ourselves, or more deeply engrossed in anything, than when we are at play."

CHARLES SCHAEFER

Becoming The Playful Leader will be fraught with challenges, but the good news is that progress is on your side. Fun is a still a grassroots movement in the workplace, and with more leaders like you realizing the potential of play, hopefully it will integrate into more and more companies and workplaces all over America.

You live in a world that has been too serious for too long. It is time to balance out the serious side of things with laughter, fun, and enjoyment. You may be afraid that you will be alone at the top, but look at it this way: if they laugh at you, that's half the battle!

Establishing Your Play Rules: Written and Unwritten

Just a couple of months ago a colleague of mine suffered a heart attack and underwent quadruple bypass heart surgery. After a successful surgery, my friend, Kim, is doing well. Here is an email he sent yesterday to a group that he leads.

"All– In the immortal words of Jack Nicholson, 'I'm back' (name the movie and you win a seat at the head of the table right in front of the candy dish at next week's meeting). We will be meeting today at 4:00 in the Academy Room of the Noyes Building. Attached below is the tentative agenda. I would like to thank Ken for filling in for me while I was gone. I would like to dispel the rumor that Ken was taking over because my 'heart' was not in it anymore. It is good to be back. – Kim."

Even rebounding from a life-threatening surgery, Kim chose to be playful and extend the invitation to each of us to do the same. What a powerful life lesson and the principle of play at its finest. Play is especially good for these tough situations because it defuses tension and puts people at ease.

To become The Playful Leader in a serious world, you need to bring playfulness closer to you when these "serious" things in life happen. At work, you should establish your play rules—the written and unwritten kind.

- Get your team involved,[41] or make it a game—and set some logical rules about play to limit any negative consequences of it in the workplace. Push the play boundaries, and chase your curiosity.
- When you innovate your own play principles, you get to establish and discuss the reason for each rule, which means

---

41 Teams That Play Together Work Together, http://www.innovativeteambuilding.co.uk/pages/articles/play.htm

that people will take it to heart. No overtly aggressive play, for example, can need some definition and brainstorming.

- Encourage your teams and employees to "play outside the lines"—in other words, to push the boundaries of what we believe can be done with play. Extend the play that works, and abolish play that is interruptive. Test live play sessions in your office, and collect results to see what works best.
- Spend some time sharing stories about play so that you can build your own set of play rules. Get top management involved, but also hear from people in the mailroom. After all, everyone matters. They all need to be happy.

Fun With Managers, Peers, and Customers

Fun has a way of trickling down and filtering into every part of business, which is an amazing thing to see. I like to think of it like one of those fancy champagne towers that you see at weddings. Champagne gets poured into a glass on the top, which overflows and fills the glasses below until eventually even the champagne glasses at the bottom are full.

In the same way, play can be implemented by you, The Playful Leader, by slowly overflowing down to your management teams, your employees, and eventually your customers. This is how you end up having a real playful culture. When your customers like you and they expect play from you, this is when you know you have reached the final glasses.

And you know what they say about glasses that are half full or half empty? Fill them up! Right now everyone is laboring under the false illusion that play has no place in the workplace, when this is exactly where it is most desperately needed.

- *Get your managers to join the party.* Introduce them to the idea of play, and back it up with many of the excellent examples I have given you in this book. There are hundreds of stats and thousands of case studies that support the play theory. The worst that can happen is that your business continues as it always has.

- *Get your peers to join in for accelerated play.* Even if this means building "play in a box" exercises to introduce the concept, the important thing here is to give people permission to enjoy themselves in a productive way that benefits the organization by improving and enhancing human capital investment.
- *Get your customers to indulge in your new playful culture.* The response will be incredible, and they want you to make it fun or they will forget it. Play stands out in this overly serious world of ours. It can make you different and happier, so share that experience with your customers for long-term customer relationship success.

I have seen company teams build[42] the most incredible concepts by embracing play and integrating it into many stages of their business. In some cases, customers are being harnessed for market research—teams simply invite them to a workshop—and for gamification—concepts are developed from collaboration.

This in turn enhances the ideas of the team while integrating the playful (and honest) perspectives of real customers in a friendly, fun, and collaborative environment. As you can imagine, the repercussions of this new form of doing business are powerful.

Just think of what you can do with actual staff meetings. Whereas they were once a practical alternative to work, you

---

42 Susan Abbott, Playing Games With Your Customers: Using Gamification in Concept Development, http://www.slideshare.net/sabbott/playing-games-with-your-customers-v4-l-p-feb

might even be able to glean some insights from people if you structure play into your meetings. Imagine that! Productive meetings where work actually happens! It would certainly be a huge shift in thinking for your business.

Creating Your Own Luck

Last summer I was driving up Canyon Road, and I noticed two young boys selling lemonade. I thought to myself—"If they are still there on my return trip, I am going to stop and give them 25 cents to help them out. Besides, I am thirsty." I learned two things that day.

As I was passing by the same location, to my delight, the boys were still there. I pulled up and said, "How's it going? What are you selling?" The response I got was, "Lemonade." I volleyed back, "How much?" The same boy paused and said, "A dollar or two." A dollar or two—are you kidding me? What does that mean?

Is he saying, "If you are cheap, you will pay us one dollar, and if you are generous, you will pay us two?" So here are my lessons. The first thing that I learned was that the price of lemonade has skyrocketed since my day. If I had bought stocks in lemons back then, I would be a rich man. The second thing I learned was that kids are getting smarter.

Or did they just "stumble" on the power of influence through social psychology tactics? Either way, they were smart. And by the time they come to work for you, they will be even smarter. These seven-year-old boys were creating their own luck.

A big part of managing a stressed, exhausted, and on-the-go workforce is not to help them with time management but to assist them with energy renewal. We create our own luck.

The Relentless Pursuit of Productive Play

I love to play, and I love to have fun. In many ways you could say that I try to instill a relentless pursuit of productive play in my business. This is because I have experienced the enormous benefits of play, and I know just how real the results are. And now I want to share it with others.

Imagine what company teams could achieve if instead of grinding all day, they stopped, looked at new models and data, and invested serious dedication, commitment, and time into the happiness and motivations of their employees. That is the world that I want to live in!

- Play has a ripple effect. When you are playful at work, it makes your employees happier. They go home and are happier with their families. Kids grow up happier because their parents were not stressed vegetables all the time. But more than that, the benefits ripple to your customers, who return the investment a thousand times.
- As a playful leader, you will have the influence to make things change. By being the core model at first, then spreading your message to others—getting management on board and eventually reshaping your business culture—you can extend and enlarge the play that you teach others for positive change and success in business.
- Part of the relentless pursuit of play involves identifying and nurturing game changers—and these will crop up more and more as you investigate different forms of play. Remember, play can be done during work, not just around work. In fact, play can improve work speed, efficiency, and competency if you let it.

- Technology[43] is your best friend because it will help you share this important new business culture with your teams. Plus, you will be able to track and measure the impact of your new structures and models, which will prove to your bosses that you are creating positive change in the company.

Your company really needs to consider playing to produce, not striving to survive. It reminds me of that sleep deprivation study I spoke about earlier. The basketball coach was doing everything—everything imaginable—to improve his team but with little luck. Training was there, routines were there, and skill building and management—all great.

Eventually he discovered that he could rapidly improve their accuracy by making them get more rest. With ten hours of sleep, the entire team became more efficient. And this is the blind spot that so many companies have. They do not realize that "adding" more to their teams will not fix the issue, because the issue is related to "lack of play and lack of rest."

A little extra fun can kick your company into high gear. Now you just need to prove it by instituting the strategies and theories that you have unearthed in this book. You will be the driver that promotes change.

Mindset, Skill Set, and Toolset: Games for the Mind

The Chicago O'Hare airport is named the "World's busiest airport." So a small town boy (me) rolled into the sprawling Chicago O'Hare airport. Flying in on a smaller regional jet put us right on the tarmac, where we had to walk to the terminals.

---

43   L Galarneau, Productive Play: Participation and Learning in Digital Game Environments, http://www.academia.edu/3382955/Productive_Play_Journal_Article_

We walked a fair distance down that tarmac, up the stairs, down the hall, and through the door into the rush of travelers.

The time was short, and I needed to find my connecting flight really quickly. I knew the airport must be large when the gate I was looking for was F1C. It sounded complicated and far away. I needed help! Upon finding the first knowledgeable employee, I said, "I am in a hurry; can you please help me find gate F1C?"

She smiled, pointed over my shoulder, and said, "It is right behind you." Sometimes we have to open our eyes and see what is standing right behind us (or in front). In this case, my story is an analogy for your workforce. All of those minds just waiting to be engaged!

The tragedy is that these individuals have spent years working without ever engaging their minds or really contributing to the success of your company. Sure, they do their jobs—but what about the three critical development paths? Forget to work on mindset, skill set and toolset with your employees and their minds will become disengaged.

- Productive play can help improve the mindset of your employees, which is important for overall happiness, job satisfaction, and performance. Introduce your employees to the idea of a "growth mindset"[44] and help them become the best versions of themselves.
- Games can help improve skills as well. In fact, many companies are using console- and PC-based games already to train their staff and develop higher functions. David Wortly, Director of the Serious Games Institute,[45]

---

44 Eleanor O'Rourke, Brain Points: A Growth Mindset Incentive Structure Boosts Persistence in an Educational Game, http://www.stanford.edu/dept/psychology/cgi-bin/drupalm/system/files/brainpoints_chi.pdf

45 Justin Richards, Serious Games Help Develop Business Skills, http://www.computerweekly.com/feature/Serious-games-help-develop-business-skills

- advocates using electronic games for business education and the development of important business skill sets.
- Games can also be essential tools for business growth that your employees need to be aware of. Think of big data systems and how they will track and measure how you do business in the future. They go beyond mind games and see your employees as the functional asset that is central to your success.

It always amazes me how blind companies can be to obvious improvements—but people resist change. Until you make play part of their lives and place it on the radar, they may go on believing that work is serious business. Of course, after reading this book, you know that something has to give.

Eventually play will have to make a come-back, or people will become a rare commodity for your company. Work and play is life. With people spending more time at work, it is about time that someone said, "Hey, why are we not enjoying our time here?" It is a valid question that your employees want answers to.

10 Principles for Integrating Work and Fun

There are ten principles that I want to share with you that will help you integrate work and fun together. It can be challenging to overcome that resistance in the beginning, but people will thank you if you see it through to the end.

#1: People follow influence. That is why you need to be playful as their leader—so that they will know that it is all right and will follow your lead. Focus on other leaders first and get your management teams to adopt the philosophy; they will love it.

#2: The best play sometimes involves winning. Competition is a natural attraction method for getting people to switch from work to play. Work is already competitive, but when you integrate fun and incentives, it can get that "play" feeling in the door.

#3: Start where you are. Everyone's starting point is different, but you always have the power to incorporate small amounts of fun into your daily team work. Make small changes, like placing hoops above trashcans or hosting a flapjack Friday.

#4: Every single day is game day, so play at your highest level. Begin educating those around you about the benefit of fun at work. Play games during your day to set an example, and watch how quickly others are interested in what you are doing.

#5: Seize playground moment opportunities. As you venture around the office, take advantage of playground moments to lighten the mood, entertain people, and connect with them. The more they like you, the higher your chances of getting them to play.

#6: Inspire play by getting small teams to play around the office. Transform a work duty into a game, and make it fun for the teams involved. Get them to provide feedback, and show this feedback to other people in the company.

#7: Go at your own speed. Depending on your business culture, your company may seize on the change to institute productive play, or they may be highly resistant to it. You need to allow your employees to eventually make a stand and say that they want the new culture.

#8: Make sure that your employees hold each other accountable so that you do not have to. This will keep the system safe, controlled, and out from under strict boss–employee work structures that cause fear and panic.

#9: Accelerate growth by making play part of your culture, not your strategy. Culture is about how things are done in general and what people believe in; strategy is just another work process. All it takes is one team to make other teams love play.

#10: Do not force play on anyone. Work to play integrations may at first cause alarm and stress. You need to educate your teams that they do not have an obligation to take part, but they have a mandate to try to relax and have fun.

Behind Enemy Lines: For Those That Don't Wanna Play

Owen Morse and John Wee met in 1986 at a juggling convention and instantly knew that they were destined to be a team. They both decided to graduate from college first. Rather than pursue careers in economics and psychology, they lit some torches and started throwing stuff into the air. Things clicked.

They have now appeared on television and in movies. Corporate entertainment and keynote speaking engagements are their normal. Not only do they entertain but they customize their performances according to what the company sells. They juggle their products, incorporate their slogans, and inspire people to build better teams.

I saw "Passing Zone" perform in Dallas at the ASTD conference in 2013. Now, these guys knew all about serious productive play and how it works. But not everyone understands or is willing to understand how play could improve their lives.

Some people are completely closed to the idea and refuse to entertain the notion. When you go behind enemy lines, things can get choppy. There are always people that point blank do not want to play. They do not laugh at jokes. They do not want to engage or take part in anything that causes so much as a cracked smile. They can be intimidating.

As in any situation when your employees are being non-compliant, it is important to defuse the tension with humor and allow the "resistant" employee to remove themselves from the experience, if that is what they want. This could happen for many reasons.

- Perhaps the employee is not resistant to play, but they are burnt out, overworked, and stressed and cannot invite anything new into their lives right now. These employees see play as just another work structure or something they "have to do."
- If the employee makes it clear that they will never play, and they strongly disapprove of the whole idea, they can be spoken to in private and educated. If this still does not work, you can grant them permission to work without play.

There is no leader in the world that will refuse something that rapidly improves productivity, revenue, and customer service. I have yet to encounter a boss so sour that he refuses to even look at the data. There is always a way in because humor is on your side.

The Power of Nurturing Game Changers

There is an opportunity gap that opens up when you first start influencing the behavior of people that work for you with play. Changing a business landscape so completely is incredibly difficult. You will figure that out when you start to try to change things.

That is why you need the help of game changers. I love game changers because they exist in every company. These individuals are open-minded, highly intelligent, and incredibly capable, and they will help you prove that play converts. You are a game changer!

Creating these "ah-ha!" moments only happens when you have a real team that is working to prove or assert that play has a place in your working environments. Even more than that, they will have to prove that play has a place in their company.

These "big idea" people are all over the place. It is your job to identify them in your company and recruit them for your play purposes. The best leaders actively pursue game changers[46] because they help you "change the game"!

Amazing people like Richard Branson and Jeff Bezos did not just stumble on big ideas and make them work by a fluke; they were committed to finding people that could help them institute and test their ideas in a real world environment. These leaders were the drivers of change, but it was the game changers that really caused the movement.

- Game changers will help you relentlessly pursue your goal of changing your company's culture into a culture of play.
- Game changers will help you come up with original, brand-centric play ideas that will suit your people and result in the conversions that you know you can get.
- Game changers will help you develop a clear purpose and plan for rolling out your playful culture in the organization. They will be your back up for when the higher ups want to know who is so "taken" with these play ideas.
- Game changers tend to enhance, extend, and leverage existing relationships so that greater emphasis can be placed on play culture with the people in your office. These are the "mini leaders" in the trenches that will become the managers of tomorrow.

Of course, a game changer does not always have to be a person. It can also be an idea created by a group of people. Think about the Google slides. You have to wonder who came up with that idea and how they proved to their managers that it worked. They obviously did a great job because now each and every Google office in the world has one.

---

46   Mike Myatt, 6 Steps for Creating a Game Changer, http://www.forbes.com/sites/mikemyatt/2012/10/10/how-great-leaders-create-game-changers/

The only thing that can result in positive change is a game changer or a larger group of people that believe in a big idea. When this happens, you will see budgets open up for you, and employees will love to see the ideas come to life.

Where and When to Play at Work

It can be difficult determining the rules of where and when you are allowed to play at work. But you should always play now so that you do not have to pay later. The payment involves slower productivity; grumpier, disengaged employees; and bad customer service. I do not even want to get into the sick days, health concerns, and stress issues.

Your job as The Playful Leader will be to help your company define where and when it is all right to play at work. This can be done when you consider the following:

- Work and play should be one and the same. There should be ways to work while playing, and there should be ways to play while also working.
- Work can happen for a while with short play breaks in between. Microsoft blares happy music and encourages dancing for a few minutes at a certain time each day because it breaks the monotony. Decide where and how your short breaks will happen. Break room? Chats? Activities?
- The where is simple if you have embraced the concept of the playful business culture. Play is an atmosphere, which means that there should be dedicated rooms where you can go and relax or engage in a play activity. There should also be smaller ways to play around the office for mundane tasks (like the hoop above the trashcan idea).
- Amplify fun by transforming basic work-related moments into moments of play. Infuse meetings with play-based

team work, and when you give speeches, use humor. Bring a humor first aid kit to work, and keep a laughter log or a humor bulletin board.

The when is a little more complicated,[47] but really, it comes down to the rules that you have set, what your teams want, and what your management is happy with. If giving your teams a break during the day improves productivity by far, then there is no reason not to embrace that metric—even if it does make the stuffed shirts grind their teeth.

I would also wholeheartedly encourage you to make spaces in your office more fun by changing the names on doors, creating fun job titles, and when you put together fun theme days or events, come up with imaginative titles to share with the world. People love different, and they enjoy looking forward to experiences even more than that.

Begin by looking for easy opportunities to introduce humor. See if you can make them permanent. Spread the ideology, and get everyone involved. Soon your entire office culture will flip, and people will love coming to work again!

The Power of Technology for Play

Technology is a huge game changer for play and one of the most incredible motivators that will prove to your bosses that play is transformational and beneficial. Think of all of the incredible inventions of the last twenty years.

There have been massive advances in mobile technology, graphics, 3D, gaming, coding, and design that have brought the virtual world into the real world. With augmented reality and hologram technology, soon the two might even be the same thing.

---

47 Martin Kimeldorf, Balancing Your Work and Play Ethics, http://www.tmsworldwide.com/kimeldorf.html

PLAY

There is real power in technology for play at work. This is especially true for Gen Ys, a critical part of the workforce, who have grown up on games and demand entertainment when they are working. More Gen Ys flock to modern companies because of things like gamification and making their average work days a fun challenge.

- Your playful culture will institute a different workplace approach, where games become central to performance. Employees will remain engaged, enthusiastic, and committed, which will help organizational goal attainment *and* improve job satisfaction and retention while reducing sick days.
- In the past, businesses dangled incentives (carrots) to motivate employees, but the system was driven by punishment if they failed. Often if targets were not met, people would be fired. Simple work became difficult because of ever-increasing targets. Nowhere is this more apparent than in call centers today.
- Gamification[48] has stepped in (the use of digital media and games for nongame activities like work, scoreboards, or challenges) and changed all of that. Now call center agents can play a game that keeps a running scoreboard as they work. It makes monotonous work fun and improves the customer experience.[49]

A recent MTV work survey proved that Millennials want their jobs to reflect their lifestyles and who they are as people. Play and games help them do just that. Education, combined

---

48   Patrick Jagoda, Gamification and Other Forms of Play, http://boundary2.dukejournals.org/content/40/2/113.abstract

49   Leonard Klie, Gamification Comes to the Contact Center, http://www.destinationcrm.com/Articles/Editorial/Magazine-Features/Gamification-Comes-to-the-Contact-Center-93677.aspx

with technology and productive play, produces workplace environments that are far more appealing—and performance centric—than they have ever been.

Technology is a big motivator, and with 25%[50] of the workforce made up of Gen Ys already, it is a strategy that your company will want to consider in the near future. Gamification can be used to orient new employees in your culture, and it can be used to train them, motivate them, teach them, and educate them—or help them achieve additional dreams.

The Play to Product Model

Products are central to the life of any business. I am talking about the products and services that your company sells to make money. Every business has them, and they are the reason you have a job to go to in the mornings.

One of my favorite benefits of play is its ability to bring different minds together. Creativity is a commodity that companies cannot afford to dismiss moving forward. And as I have explained, creativity and innovation are darn near impossible without regular play.

- Product and service development do not just belong to research and development teams anymore. This is an old siloed practice. Instead, allow any employee that works in your company to contribute.
- When you use play as a structure for conceptualization and brainstorming, you bring multiple minds and perspectives together for the improvement of your products and services. Imagine how much better your business would be if everyone cared about the things you were selling!

---

50 Eric Savitz, Let's Play: To Keep Gen Y Staffers, Gamify Their Work, http://www.forbes.com/sites/ciocentral/2012/07/03/lets-play-to-keep-gen-y-staffers-gamify-their-work/

I like to call this the "play-to-product" model because it results in a new product. Many "ah-ha!" moments happen after or during play, which makes playful teams far more accurate at coming up with different ideas than teams bound to work and work alone.

Products are important, and with rising competition and online sales, only the companies that utilize their entire employee workforce will benefit in the end. The rest will continue to sink millions into product development, keeping that narrow focus—unable to see the potential in different perspectives or ideas. Why not divert some of that *change* into productive play?

I would encourage you to always invite as many employees as are willing to engage in product development workshops and play sessions. These can be astoundingly beneficial, and they can even solve problems that normal R&D teams have had for years.

You will end up delivering better, faster service and will increase customer satisfaction across the board, which is great for repeat sales. The best side effect, however, will be that your employees are finally valued and able to affect your company in positive ways.

They do not have to stick to their job description but instead can contribute as a whole to the many processes, systems, products, and services that need to grow in your company. This will make them feel valuable, which in turn will translate into stronger brand bonds, loyalty, and commitment.

Playing to produce a product that will sell is often exactly the kind of outside-the-box thinking that leads to breakthroughs. In these unstable economic times, your company can certainly use the competitive advantage of play-to-product models.

After all, is not business a game that we are all just playing anyway? You play in exchange for money. Your boss plays to win.

Competition is everywhere, so it might as well work for your benefit in productive ways.

Putting Together Your Business Play Approach

A time will come when you have influenced enough people to get a foot in the door. Perhaps senior management has given you the go ahead to conduct a trial play program. Whatever your motivation, you will need to put together a business play approach.

You are not trying to survive, you are attempting to thrive – so you have to be creative and think outside the box for your play approach. Think about the following things, and host a meeting where you can appoint a fun squad or a dedicated play manager to help you.

- What will the company allow you to do?
- How far can you stretch the boundaries of the rules they have given you?
- What will go inside your business play kit?
- Who will take part in your initial play trials?

Imagine walking into the office with a suitcase. Inside that suitcase is everything you need to begin a playful culture at work. You have recruited the right teams and people are being influenced by your playful behavior. The next step is to roll out your approach.

Building Your Brilliant Ideas Checklist

A brilliant ideas checklist is an ongoing document that helps you keep track of play opportunities that you could institute in your company. To begin with, you first need to conduct a play assessment. How much does your company already play? From

PLAY

there, you can move on to newer, better ideas to enhance and revamp your business culture.

- The best ideas in the world are recycled. Take a look at other models of adult play, and see if they inspire you to create an atmosphere or an activity that will be appreciated and enjoyed by your workforce.
- Remember that all play ideas must serve a function or purpose. This is productive play after all! Assign a purpose to each and every play structure.
- Host meetings in different departments and see what they want to do with play. Sometimes you get the most interesting ideas from the most unlikely places. Break down walls and investigate across departments.
- Host meetings with your senior management teams, and give them a "wow" presentation on what you would like to institute in the company. Show them real ideas, structures, and models from the world that other companies are using.
- A checklist should contain ideas from everywhere, so do not forget the smaller jobs—like the cleaners, the coffee runners, the assistants, and the technical staff. These employees make your job possible, and they could use play in their jobs most of all because their jobs are the most repetitive and mundane.

To build a brilliant ideas checklist, you will have to transform the ideas of your people into actionable goals. Try to match them to budgets and resources, and see if permission would be granted for your many suggestions.

These will keep coming, so you may end up with a document that continually needs to be updated or a folder that keeps growing in size. Get your data analysts involved, and give them something exciting to do.

Also take some time to explore other playful organizations and how they make their workplaces fun. You may not even realize it, but a play structure could be leading all the best talent to them! Analyze their structures, and then see if you can improve on them.

Mondays will never be the same again if you can get your checklist right. There will always be new programs to try, old ones to measure, and events to enjoy. This is what makes a modern business thrive. But it is also something that has to be tested to be truly believed.

Amplify your fun, and keep it going by building a brilliant checklist with the input from competitors and everyone in your business. Take all opinions into account; after all, they are the people who need play the most.

Assessing and Measuring Play Structures in Business

By now, I hope that you are convinced that the power of productive play is amazing. It is more than just the future; it is our present! To play is profitable. It changes behavior and helps people connect with each other. Play inspires collective genius—a genius that you can put to work for the benefit of everyone in your company. Play changes everything.

There are not many things more business relevant than play. It is completely absent from most business models, which is a travesty. The dividends of play can significantly enhance the quality of every relationship in every level of your life.

How can instant improvements and instant happiness not be your top priority? Every day you are witness to the harsh effects of lower pay, higher stress levels, and a greater need to compete with companies that seem to pull success out of nowhere. Well, now you understand that nowhere is actually a place of fun. You need to get there, quickly!

Play structures can and should be changed, altered, and revamped every so often. Keep it fresh, and keep your employees guessing. Remember, it is not only about play around work but play during work as well.

Present your findings to your bosses, and revel in the success that you deserve. Play is the future, and it is the saving grace for many people that struggle to make it to work every day, because they are so emotionally and physically exhausted. Save them!

> **THE PLAYFUL LEADER WILL**
> - *Articulate Your Culture Of Play*
> - *Radiate Your Playful Attitude*
> - *Demonstrate Your Playful Nature*
> - *Validate Your Game Changers*
> - *Escalate Your Playful Culture*

---

8 Fun Ideas to Get You Started

For your own company, you will have to feel what can be done and take note of what people do not like to find the right balance in your play structures. Here are ten of the best ideas that I use regularly when giving seminars and conferences.

#1: Train new employees in your cultural values by giving them a list of things that they need to know and sending them on an exciting scavenger hunt. During this journey, they will need to meet key people and interact with veteran employees.

#2: Incorporate humor into training sessions. Use props and jokes, and get people to engage with the lessons that you are

teaching them through play. It reduces anxiety and improves their ability to learn.

#3: Host friendly yet bold competitions and events between departments. This will promote collaboration and pull departments together. Keep changing the themes so no department is able to dominate and feel superior to other departments.

#4: Some of your workplace policies should state "fun," outrageous things; you can also add humor to your email signatures, and you should fund staff photos to promote unity. There should be a "normal" photo and a crazy one for the walls every year.

#5: Form a fun committee, and put them in charge of a budget. Allow them to do whatever they like with it as long as it entertains and adds fun to the office environment.

#6: Amplify the fun in the company by involving everyone in a large activity at least once a month to build commitment and employee friendships and promote collaboration. The music at Microsoft is an example of an overall play structure.

#7: Assign fun to individuals that really enjoy it. Allow them to make suggestions on events and experiences for the whole office. These individuals make meetings interesting, as they will seize the opportunity to play.

#8: Keep people and the play they love at the heart of your organization. Create a large employee wall where everyone has a place. Allow people to decorate their workstations, and free them to express who they are in the way that they dress, work, and play.

Conclusion

The Playful Leader is an individual that leads by example. With influence, knowledge, and an appreciation for the positive benefits of fun and play in the workplace, you can create positive change in your organization.

All you have to do is acknowledge The Playful Leader Matrix and identify the types of people in your office and how they would want to play—so that you can build play structures and models for them that will work.

From there, it is a simple matter of allowing the "trickle down" effect to happen. Once people see that you have given them permission to play, they will begin to spread the message and play themselves.

Eventually, your business culture will change from stiff, hard, and boring to relaxed, fun, and creative (oh, and profitable). Any business can experience the benefits of play, and employees need this kind of consideration to be happy in their work.

As The Playful Leader, you will singlehandedly transform your employees into game changers and ignite a new play revolution in your company. When your bosses see the increases in productivity, revenue, health, happiness, and performance of your employees, they will soon come around to your dynamic way of doing business.

You will have to reinvent the standard for business wherever you are. Ask yourself how you can change things. Give everyone the tools they need to implement this change! There are a number of things that need to be brought together, so you will need relentless passion to make things happen.

This system will show you how to build great, playful teams through a variety of techniques—all aimed at taking a winning team to the next level. We want to mobilize a group of people around a set of values and a mission that drives the enterprise to new levels to make ordinary people do extraordinary things! All of this comes together in this methodology.

Take these principles and decide to change lives. Change organizational direction. Change culture. Games are directed by rules. The traditional rules of business culture need to change so that your results change too.

The one thing that has been missing from our lives for so long has been play. It is a need that cannot be ignored anymore. There is simply too much competition, stress, and panic in companies today that needs to be sorted out.

Convert your employees into happy people, and see how much more they will appreciate working for you. The results are significant and long lasting, and your customers will be the ones that truly benefit the most. It is a win–win and an absolute must these days.

When you learn to see and identify play in the world, you are inspired to commit to that change. Change what you aspire to be—learn, innovate, and share. Decide to create a learning environment within the culture of your organization. Understand that you do not have all the answers. No one has all the answers. Come to the party—bring the issues and questions, and then build upon what you do know.

You are creating a way of life that goes beyond business. This culture is a way of life. Your job as a manager is to lead by example and to give your employees permission to play. To give this permission is to empower your people. Give them authority to act in a playful manner.

All change starts within. So first change yourself and become empowered. Then as a leader in modern society, give your people permission to engage in productive play. This is a different definition on how we run our businesses. It is a shift in culture, in how we do business, and in how we live to be a game changer of the future. Define the behaviors you want your people to exhibit. Hear the voices of everyone in the game. Get the best ideas on the table, and make collective decisions so that you can move forward.

And then take your idea to a bigger audience. Teach aspiring managers how to do it. Practice and tell them how it works. Be committed to delivering play. While you are at it, deliver profits. Productive play is good for business! The exciting thing is that you can increase the depth and scale of your influence as The Playful Leader.

Become The Playful Leader by implementing the cultural changes and techniques that you have learned in this book. Share your playfulness with others, and inspire real change in ailing companies that cannot figure out why everyone is so unhappy.

This is your time to shine. You have to be The Playful Leader your company deserves, not the one they think they need.

Play changes everything—everyone wins!

Super-Charge Your Playful Leader Development with Engaging Keynotes and Workshops

Bring the Playful Leader Workshop to Your Organization. Develop Playful Leaders throughout your company or team with the Playful Leader Workshop. This adaptable workshop comes in 90 minute, half day, and full day formats. This fast-paced, interactive training will delight your organization and introduce game changing tactics that will lead to higher levels of achievement. Organizations of all sizes have experienced Russ' playful passion and the energy he radiates from the get-go.

Bring Russ Johnson to Your Next Meeting, Conference, or Event. Russ delivers dynamite keynotes that engage and inspire your organization in a fun and playful (of course) way. You will feel and see the energy that exudes during the presentation. You will witness first-hand what this new leadership secret is all about. It truly does change everything. See transformative play at its finest, and learn how to create your own.

To learn more, or inquire about availability, please visit www.ThePlayfulLeader.com, or email at capturetraining@gmail.com.

We Need Your Help

If you have been inspired by The Playful Leader philosophy in this book and want to help others awaken The Playful Leader within, here are some action steps you can take immediately to make a positive difference:

- Gift *PLAY: The New Leadership Secret That Changes Everything* to coworkers, friends, and family members. Give the gift of play to inspire, lift, and encourage others to greater levels of achievement and happiness. It will be an appreciated gift that will ignite The Playful Leader in others to manage more effectively and embrace change.
- Share your thoughts about this book on Twitter, Facebook, LinkedIn, and the websites that you visit. If you have your own website, you can blog about *PLAY: The New Leadership Secret That Changes Everything* or write a book review.
- If you are a business owner or manager, you can invest in copies of this book so all of your teammates learn to be The Playful Leader and achieve peak performance.

- Help each of the members of your organization become The Playful Leader so that you all succeed in these times of regular change.
- Ask your local newspaper, radio station, or online media outlets to have the author interviewed to share how everyone can be The Playful Leader at work and in life and, in turn, make it more enjoyable.
- To book a Playful Leader keynote presentation or training for your team with Russ Johnson or one of his certified trainers, please contact The Playful Leader Group at www.ThePlayfulLeader.com.

References

Chapter 1

Darley, Susan Ann, *12 Mind-Blowing Benefits Of Play – Including At Work,* http://www.awaken.com/2013/06/12-mind-blowing-benefits-of-play-including-at-work/

Weisenthal, Joe, *Check Out How Much The Average American Works Each Year Compared To The French, The Germans, And The Koreans,* http://www.businessinsider.com/average-annual-hours-worked-for-americans-vs-the-rest-of-the-world-2013-8

Building Morale In The Workplace, http://www.uwinnipeg.ca/hr/benefits/docs/efap/hw_feb_09.pdf

Heracleous, Loizos, and Jacobs, Claus, *The Serious Business Of Play,* http://sloanreview.mit.edu/article/the-serious-business-of-play/

Vorhauser-Smith, Sylvia, *How The Best Places To Work Are Nailing Employee Engagement,* http://www.forbes.com/sites/sylviavorhausersmith/2013/08/14/how-the-best-places-to-work-are-nailing-employee-engagement/

Zappos Family Core Value #3, Create Fun And A Little Weirdness, http://about.zappos.com/our-unique-culture/zappos-core-values/create-fun-and-little-weirdness

Spektor, Dina, *11 Ways Playing Video Games Makes You Smarter And Healthier,* http://business.financialpost.com/2013/09/14/11-ways-playing-video-games-makes-you-smarter-and-healthier/

Chapter 2

Ford, Robert C, McLaughlin, Frank S, Newstrom, John W, *Questions And Answers About Fun At Work*, http://www.highbeam.com/doc/1G1-113564466.html

Penn State, *Fun At Work Promotes Employee Retention But May Hurt Productivity*, http://www.sciencedaily.com/releases/2013/11/131121135633.htm

Tarkan, Laurie, *Work Hard, Play Harder: Fun At Work Boosts Creativity, Productivity*, http://www.foxnews.com/health/2012/09/13/work-hard-play-harder-fun-at-work-boosts-creativity-productivity/

Vong, Katherine, *5 Ways To Boost Creativity In The Workplace*, http://www.trendreports.com/article/boost-creativity-in-the-workplace

Wilson, Steve, *Play Improves Morale And Productivity*, http://www.worldlaughtertour.com/pdfs/04%20Play%20Improves%20morale.pdf

Chapter 4

Null, Christopher, *Does Gaming At Work Improve Productivity?* http://www.pcworld.com/article/155284/gamingatwork.html

Gargiulo, Susanne, *Play To Win: Work Games Can Give A Career Power-UP*, http://edition.cnn.com/2013/02/27/business/work-simulation-games-route-to-the-top/

Blue Ridge Bank, Serious Banking, http://www.seriousplay.com/18045/BLUE%20RIDGE%20BANK

Stambor, Zak, *How Laughing Leads To Learning*, http://www.apa.org/monitor/jun06/learning.aspx

McGhee, Paul, PhD, *Humor Helps Produce An Emotionally Intelligent Workplace*, http://www.laughterremedy.com/article_pdfs/Emotional%20Intelligence.pdf

Cori, *Having Fun At Work Pays Off*, http://bvblog.baudville.com/post/2010/08/26/Having-Fun-at-Work-Pays-Off.aspx#.U3842PmSySo

Chapter 5

Brainy Quote, Play Quotes, http://www.brainyquote.com/quotes/keywords/play.html

Gupta, Traveen, *Fear Or Fun At Work*, http://www.qualitydigest.com/inside/six-sigma-column/fear-or-fun-work

Tartakovsky, Margarita, MS, *The Importance Of Play For Adults*, http://psychcentral.com/blog/archives/2012/11/15/the-importance-of-play-for-adults/

Economy, Peter, *5 Things You Must Do To Keep Your Best People*, http://www.inc.com/peter-economy/5-things-you-must-do-to-keep-your-best-people.

Kaplan, Soren, *6 Ways To Create A Culture Of Innovation*, http://www.fastcodesign.com/1672718/6-ways-to-create-a-culture-of-innovation

Pelle, *The Piano Stairs of Fun Theory – Short Run Fun And Not A Nudge*, http://www.inudgeyou.com/the-piano-stairs-of-fun-theory-short-run-fun-and-not-a-nudge/

Stepper, John, Applying The Fun Theory At Work, http://johnstepper.com/2013/02/02/applying-the-fun-theory-at-work/

Lynley, Matt, *Ranked: The Best Slides And Worst Slides In Google's Offices*, http://www.businessinsider.com/googles-office-slides-2012-5?op=1

Six Cool Companies To Work For, http://www.cnbc.com/id/39573304/page/5

Cavale, Siddharth, *Best Buy Profit Beats Estimates, Shows Signs Of Turnaround*, http://www.reuters.com/article/2014/05/22/us-bestbuy-results-idUSBREA4LoCM20140522

Chapter 6

Brainy Quote, Play Quotes, http://www.brainyquote.com/quotes/keywords/play.html

Goldstein Graham, Lisa, *What Is It Like To Be Funny?* https://etd.ohiolink.edu/rws_etd/document/get/antioch1275056868/inline

Richardson, Rachel, *The Utility Of Humor In Leadership Communication,* https://www.lycoming.edu/schemata/pdfs/CCOM_RRichardson.pdf

Mc Innis, Jan, *4 Ways To Use Self-Deprecating Humor,* http://comedywriterblog.com/4-ways-to-use-self-deprecating-humor/

Wylie, Ian, *More Play, More Work,* http://www.theguardian.com/money/blog/2009/jan/07/playing-games-at-work

Kashdan, Todd, *The Power Of Curiosity,* http://experiencelife.com/article/the-power-of-curiosity/

Singh, Gunjan, *Impact Of Playing With Imaginary Worlds On Adult Creativity,* http://www.examiner.com/article/impact-of-playing-with-imaginary-worlds-on-adult-creativity

Wenner, Melinda, *The Serious Need For Play,* http://www.scientificamerican.com/article/the-serious-need-for-play/

Chalufour, Ingrid, Drew, Walter F, Waite-Stupiansky, Sandi, *Learning To Play Again,* http://www.naeyc.org/files/yc/file/200305/ConstructWorkshops_Chalufour.pdf

Spielberger, Tracy, *All Work And No Play? There's A Better Way,* http://www.playworks.org/blog/all-work-and-no-play-there%E2%80%99s-better-way

Markowitz, Eric, *Brilliant Leaders Use This Type Of Humor (Hint: Think Woody Allen),* http://www.inc.com/magazine/201306/eric-markowitz/humor-self-deprecation-leaders.html

Chapter 7

Avala, Nick, *July Trend Report Examines 'Play As A Competitive Advantage'*, http://www.jwtintelligence.com/2012/07/july-trend-report-examines-play-competitive-advantage/#axzz32yx5Hepg

SHRM, Fun Work Environment Survey http://www.shrm.org/Research/SurveyFindings/Documents/SHRM%20Fun%20Work%20Environment%20Survey.pdf

Press Release, *Funny, They Don't Look Like Comedians,* http://www.peppercomm.com/news/press-release/funny-they-dont-look-like-comedians

Fuller, Richard Buckminster, *Quotes,* http://www.goodreads.com/author/quotes/165737.Richard_Buckminster_Fuller

Grace, Yvonne, *The Creation Spark,* http://scriptadvice.wordpress.com/2014/03/18/the-creation-spark/

Widrich, Leo, *Why We Have Our Best Ideas In The Shower: The Science Of Creativity,* http://blog.bufferapp.com/why-we-have-our-best-ideas-in-the-shower-the-science-of-creativity

Green, Charles H, *Trust And The Sharing Economy: A New Business Model,* http://trustedadvisor.com/articles/trust-and-the-sharing-economy-a-new-business-model

Chapter 8

Hoption, Collette, Barling, Julian, Turner, Nick, *"It's Not You, It's Me: Transformational Leadership And Self-Deprecating Humor,* http://www.emeraldinsight.com/journals.htm?articleid=17076800

Crace, John, *When Humour Is A Serious Business,* http://www.theguardian.com/money/2003/jan/11/workandcareers.jobsandmoney

Belkin, Lisa, *The Fun Workplace May Be The Most Productive – New York Times,* http://blog.miodragkostic.com/2008/04/

Toneguzzi, Mario, *Companies Using Humour To Grow Business, Also A Way To Attract And Retain Employees,* http://www.calgaryherald.com/business/Companies+using+humour+grow+business/9284763/story.html

Smith, Jacquelyn, *10 Reasons Why Humor Is Key To Success At Work,* http://www.forbes.com/sites/jacquelynsmith/2013/05/03/10-reasons-why-humor-is-a-key-to-success-at-work/

Romero, Eric J, PhD, *Humor...The Social Catalyst At Work,* http://competeoutsidethebox.com/wp-content/uploads/articles/Humor%20the%20Social%20Catalyst%20at%20Work.pdf

Shaw, Colin, *Using Humor In Business: Some Prctical Advice,* http://www.beyondphilosophy.com/blog/using-humor-in-business

Llopis, Glenn, *6 Ways To Make Your Leadership And Workplace Fun Again,* http://www.forbes.com/sites/glennllopis/2013/09/23/6-ways-to-make-your-leadership-and-workplace-fun-again/

Taylor, Steve, *The Secret Of Success: Relax And Do Nothing,* http://www.psychologytoday.com/blog/out-the-darkness/201401/the-secret-success-relax-and-do-nothing

Gray, Peter, *The Value Of Plat II: How Play Promotes Reasoning,* http://www.psychologytoday.com/blog/freedom-learn/200812/the-value-play-ii-how-play-promotes-reasoning

Dobson, Louise, *What's Your Humor Style?* http://www.psychologytoday.com/articles/200606/whats-your-humor-style

Gordon, Gwen, Esbjorn-Hargens, Sean, Integral Play: An Exploration Of Adult Transformation, http://www.gwengordonplay.com/pdf/integral_play.pdf

Shaw, Colin, *Using Humor In Business: Some Practical Advice,* http://www.beyondphilosophy.com/blog/using-humor-in-business

References

Chapter 9

Gilkey, Roderick, Kilts, Clint, *Cognitive Fitness,* http://hbr.org/2007/11/cognitive-fitness/ar/1

Gemma, Anthony, *Making People Smile Program,* http://www.anthonygemma.com/PDF_FunProgramLaunch.pdf

Gordon, Jon, *Positive Thinking Is Contagious,* http://www.guideposts.org/positive-thinking/power-positive-thinking-work

The Opportunities Corporate Innovation, http://www.nifplay.org/opportunities/corporate-innovation/

Nussbaum, Bruce, *How Serious Play Leads To Breakthrough Innovation,* http://www.fastcodesign.com/1671971/how-serious-play-leads-to-breakthrough-innovation

Graber, Michael, Atkinson, Jocelyn, *The Role Of Play In Innovation,* http://www.memphisdailynews.com/news/2014/jan/27/the-role-of-play-in-innovation/

Stillman, Jessica, *Forced 'Fun" At Work": Researchers Uncover A Dark Side,* http://www.cbsnews.com/news/forced-fun-at-work-researchers-uncover-a-dark-side/

Hartley, Deanna, *Forcing Fun In The Workplace? Funny How It Can Fail,* http://thehiringsite.careerbuilder.com/2014/01/31/forcing-fun-workplace/

Chapter 10

Daniels, Bryan C, *Light Humor In The Workplace Is A Good Thing, Says Mu Business Professor,* http://munews.missouri.edu/news-releases/2007/1030-robert-humor.php

Osak, Mitchell, *Gamification Unboxed: Should You Play Games With Your Customers?* http://www.callcenter-iq.com/customer-experience/articles/gamification-unboxed-should-you-play-games-with-yo/

Lerose, Robert, *Playing To Win: How Gamifying Your Customers And Employees Can Lead To Better Results,* https://smallbusinessonlinecommunity.bankofamerica.com/community/running-your-business/sales-marketing/blog/2014/05/19/playing-to-win-how-gamifying-your-customers-and-employees-can-lead-to-better-results

Anderson, Kare, *15 Ways To Accomplish More With The Right Kind Of Humor,* http://www.forbes.com/sites/kareanderson/2012/08/13/15-ways-to-accomplish-more-with-the-right-kind-of-humor/

De Masi, Casandra, *The Self-Depracating Humour Conundrum,* http://www.theargus.ca/articles/editorials/2014/01/the-self-deprecating-humour-conundrum

Hickey, Kit, Six Ideas For A More Productive Work Day, http://www.forbes.com/sites/yec/2014/01/21/six-ideas-for-a-more-productive-work-day/

Chapter 11

Brainy Quote, *Happiness,* http://www.brainyquote.com/quotes/topics/topic_happiness.html

Phillips, David, Quotes, http://www.kuote.us/quotes_book.php?idBook=112&uid=111925997467738650481

Gregoire, Carolyn, *How To Wire Your Brain For Happiness,* http://www.huffingtonpost.com/2013/10/17/how-tiny-joyful-moments-c_n_4108363.html

Achor, Shawn, *The Happiness Advantage,* http://www.jtbookyard.com/uploads/6/2/9/3/6293106/the_happiness_advantage.pdf

Tsai, Derek, *Learn By Blogging,* http://learnbyblogging.com/?p=2535

Achor, Shawn, *The Happiness Advantage: The Seven Principles Of Positive Psychology That Fuell Success And Performance,* http://

www.worldcat.org/title/happiness-advantage-the-seven-principles-of-positive-psychology-that-fuel-success-and-performance-at-work/oclc/495271368

Silverblatt, Rob, *The Science Of Workplace Happiness*, http://money.usnews.com/money/careers/articles/2010/04/14/the-science-of-workplace-happiness

Fairchild, Caroline, *Workplace Happiness Survey* Finds Friends Are More Important Than Salary, http://www.huffingtonpost.com/2012/10/17/workplace-happiness-friends-over-salary_n_1971110.html

Dishman, Lydia, Secrets of America's Happiest Companies, http://www.fastcompany.com/3004595/secrets-americas-happiest-companies

Schwartz, Tony, *Relax! You'll Be More Productive,* http://www.nytimes.com/2013/02/10/opinion/sunday/relax-youll-be-more-productive.html?pagewanted=all&_r=0

Galarnean, L, *Productive Play: Participation And Learning In Digital Game Environments,* http://www.academia.edu/3382955/Productive_Play_Journal_Article_

Hickey, Kit, *Six Ideas For a More Productive Work Day,* http://www.forbes.com/sites/yec/2014/01/21/six-ideas-for-a-more-productive-work-day/

Matous, Filip, *Can Ping Pong In The Office Increase Productivity,* http://enviableworkplace.com/can-ping-pong-in-the-office-increase-productivity/

Nauert, Rick, PhD, *Video Games Can Help Boost Social, Memory And Cognitive Skills,* http://psychcentral.com/news/2013/11/26/video-games-help-boost-social-memory-cognitive-skills/62537.html

Richards, Justin, *Serious Games Help Develop Business Skills,* http://www.computerweekly.com/feature/Serious-games-help-develop-business-skills

Stanley, Robert, *Top 25 Best Examples of Gamification In Business*, http://blogs.clicksoftware.com/clickipedia/top-25-best-examples-of-gamification-in-business/

Humour In Business, http://www.ryanandassociates.com.au/humourart5.htm

Kohrman, Miles, *10 Ways To Make Your Office More Fun*, http://www.fastcompany.com/3014585/how-to-be-a-success-at-everything/10-ways-to-make-your-office-more-fun

Stark, Peter, Barron, *What Should A Manager Do When Employees Are Not Team Players?* http://www.hirecentrix.com/what-should-a-manager-do-when-employees-are-not-team-players.html

Myatt, Mike, *6 Steps For Creating A Game Changer*, http://www.forbes.com/sites/mikemyatt/2012/10/10/how-great-leaders-create-game-changers/

Kimeldorf, Martin, *Balancing Your Work And Play Ethics*, http://www.tmsworldwide.com/kimeldorf.html

Benoni, Dan, *Gamification Of Engagement & Culture*, http://www.slideshare.net/dbenoni/gamification-of-engagement-culture

Jagoda, Patrick, *Gamification And Other Forms Of Play*, http://boundary2.dukejournals.org/content/40/2/113.abstract

Savitz, Eric, *Let's Play: To Keep Gen Y Staffers, Gamify Their Work*, http://www.forbes.com/sites/ciocentral/2012/07/03/lets-play-to-keep-gen-y-staffers-gamify-their-work/

Klie, Leonard, *Gamification Comes To The Contact Center*, http://www.destinationcrm.com/Articles/Editorial/Magazine-Features/Gamification-Comes-to-the-Contact-Center-93677.aspx

Buchanan, Scott, *Gamification: How To Power Up Your Contact Centre Staff*, http://www.mycustomer.com/feature/experience/gamification-how-power-your-contact-centre/165788

Chan Kim, W, *How Strategy Shapes Structure*, http://hbr.org/2009/09/how-strategy-shapes-structure/ar/1

About the Author

Keynote speaker, trainer, author, and teacher Russ Johnson has a Master's Degree from American Graduate School of International Management (Thunderbird) and a BA from Brigham Young University. Johnson has spoken to and trained major companies such as American Express, Disney, Weight Watchers International, Goldman Sachs, New York Life, Microsoft, Caesars Entertainment, E*Trade , and others. He has pioneered programs in Leadership, Customer Service, Engagement, Team Building, and Change Management. His focus is on learning transfer and closing the knowing–doing gap in a fun and entertaining way! ThePlayfulLeader.com

Made in the USA
San Bernardino, CA
12 October 2014